NEW INTERIORS

INSIDE 40 OF THE MOST SPECTACULAR HOMES

NEW INTERIORS

INSIDE 40 OF THE MOST SPECTACULAR HOMES

Anja Llorella Oriol

COLLINS DESIGN

An Imprint of HarperCollinsPublishers

First Edition

First published in 2006 by:
Collins Design
An *Imprint* of HarperCollins*Publishers*
10 East 53rd Street
New York, NY 10022
Tel.: (212) 207-7000
Fax: (212) 207-7654
collinsdesign@harpercollins.com
www.harpercollins.com

Distributed throughout the world by:
HarperCollins*Publishers*
10 East 53rd Street
New York, NY 10022
Fax: (212) 207-7654

Packaged by
LOFT Publications
Via Laietana, 32, 4.° Of. 92
08003 Barcelona, Spain
Tel.: +34 932 688 088
Fax: +34 932 687 073
loft@loftpublications.com
www.loftpublications.com

Editor:
Anja Llorella Oriol

Translation:
Nadja Leonard and Christian Siegmund

Art Director:
Mireia Casanovas Soley

Layout:
Oriol Serra Juncosa

Library of Congress Cataloging-in-Publication Data

Llorella, Anja.
  New interiors. Inside 40 of the most spectacular homes / Anja
Llorella Oriol. — 1st ed.
  p. cm.
  ISBN-13: 978-0-06-113972-7 (hardcover)
  ISBN-10: 0-06-113972-6 (hardcover)
  1. Interior decoration. 2. Interior architecture. 3. House
furnishings. I. Title.

NK2110.L66 2007
747—dc22

2006031546

Printed in China
First Printing, 2006

For most people, home is the nicest place to relax and unwind. However, in order to feel truly at home within one's own four walls, one needs more than just furnishings, fittings and a dynamic color scheme. One must skillfully set the scene using light, forms and surfaces. Thanks to the rise of interior design as an independent profession at the turn of the 20th century—under the influence of the English Arts and Crafts movement and the German Work Alliance—a multitude of options now exist.

Technical innovations have enabled designers to use a large palette of materials and construction methods, leading to intense and fruitful aesthetic debates. The result: multifaceted interiors in which styles, may be eclectically combined.

One of the sustained stylistic tendencies in the 20th century is the high-tech minimalism; increasingly, classic shapes and style elements historic building materials are being incorporated into minimalist environments. Furthermore, ecological issues have accelerated the adoption of natural, environmentally-friendly materials such as, wood and bamboo.

The globalization of culture also led to an exchange of ideas about flexible living concepts. Nowadays many living spaces are designed to flow into one another smoothly and to change their configuration easily by the use of sliding doors or panels. In addition, unnecessary details are forsaken, light becomes one of the primary design elements, and color assumes greater importance.

Obviously, communication with the client leads to the home design that may express the residents personality via an abundance of styles, shapes, materials and design concepts. All of the spectacular rooms presented on the following pages have one thing in common: They epitomize the idea of modern interior design—innovative yet functional and timeless at their core.

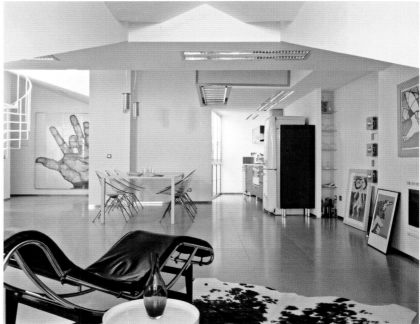

HOUSES

Y-House

Location Jingumae, Tokyo, Japan **Photography** © Ryota Atarashi, Shinkenchiku-sha

The point of departure for this single-family home in Tokyo was an unfinished structure, originally planned as a multi-family building. When the architect started the project, only the incomplete basic concrete structure existed, without shutters or interior fittings. Since the building had been designed to accommodate eight apartments, the individual rooms were small. Upon consideration, the architect, Frank la Rivière, and the owner decided to keep the building's basic structure and to enlarge rooms by removing walls. They could thereby maintain the existing concrete base and define the individual rooms with different materials and colors: bamboo for the kitchen, galvanized steel plates for the living room, vulcanized recycled paper for the guest room and padded denim for the children's room. Halogen lamps illuminate the rather closed rooms, while impressive, voluminous lighting fixtures adorn the dining and living areas.

In the kitchen and the dining area, the cladding of the concrete walls with bamboo panels creates a friendly and warm atmosphere, dressed up a touch by the elegant chandelier over the dining table.

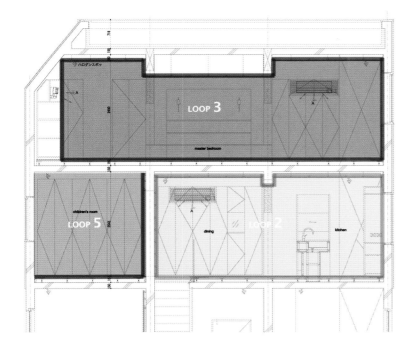

Section

Zinc-coated steel plates running over two floors define the living room. The opaque stairway cladding, broken up by circular holes, strengthens the open design concept and also creates an interesting play of light.

So that the children could play happily and safely, their room was lined with denim cushions, a striking contrast to the cool (and partially visible) concrete structure.

Ibiza House

Location Ibiza, Spain **Photography** © Jordi Miralles

This concept shows that a traditional Ibiza-style house can be updated harmoniously with contemporary elements that neither compromise nor with its traditional design vocabulary. To achieve this, the open-plan rooms were filled with modern furniture juxtaposed with traditional materials and colors. As is often the case in Mediterranean architecture, the color white dominates and the walls were covered in a limestone coating. Only decorative elements, such as paintings, carpets, and Florence furniture by Zanotta in the entrance area provide color accents in these airy and open surroundings. In this star-shaped house, the living room was designed as the center and functional axis; all additional rooms extend outward from here. The boundary between living room and dining room is established in a manner that is both elegant and functional: An oval wall unit designed by the architect serves as a room divider. The living room's importance as a focal point of the house is also emphasized in the design of the adjacent terrace, which on warm summer nights helps turn the living room into an at-home chill-out spot.

The open-plan rooms were outfitted with modern furnishings but
finished with traditional materials such as the ochre-colored floor
tiles and the white limestone wall coating.

The oval closet wall, which allows to the shape of the round table by Vitra, serves as an elegant and functional divider between the dining area and the living room.

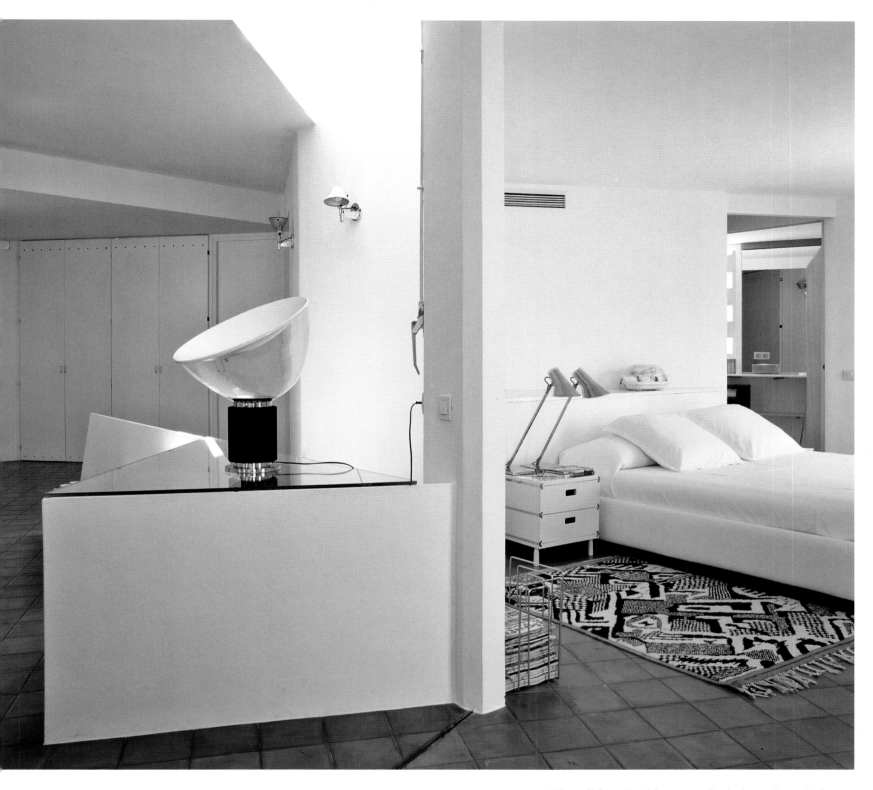

Jutting off from the living room, the bedroom has a bathroom with a sliding door. The dominant white color scheme creates a Mediterranean and almost ethereal atmosphere.

Equipped with a blue awning and modern furniture, including a
circular sofa, the atrium-like terrace lets residents and guests chill
out and enjoy Ibiza's warm summer nights in style.

Dromana Residence

Location Dromana Beach, Victoria, Australia **Photography** © Shania Shegedyn

This summery single-family house was built on a slope in Dromana, a small town on Australia's Mornington Peninsula. The long building's main body rests on a foundation of coarse fieldstones, which serves to link the house visually with its sandy surroundings. Fieldstone is is also used for the fireplace cladding in the living room, thereby creating a connection to the façade. Meanwhile, the wood used for the roofed foyer is reiterated in the interior rooms, banisters and the built-in closets, lending a cozier atmosphere to the white rooms. An open, continuous floor plan reinforces the feeling of spaciousness created by the glass façades facing the ocean; also enhancing this light-flooded environment are symmetrically designed skylights. In contrast, narrow window openings facing the street protect the rooms from too much brightness. The red entrance door and the oval recess in the foyer—a shape repeated in the interiors via an oval dividing wall—serve as elements of contrast in these simple surroundings.

To create a cozy environment in the otherwise sleek white rooms, the floors, stairway, and built-in closets were clad in wooden panels and the fireplace was given a facing of coarse fieldstones.

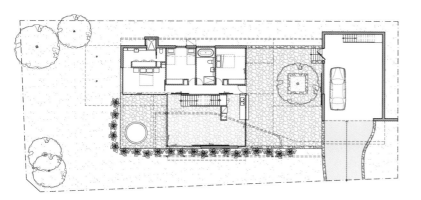

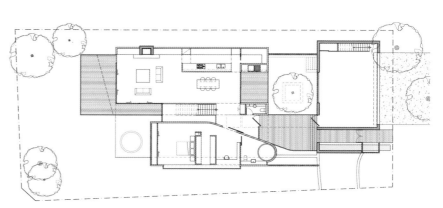

Ground floor

First floor

An oval structure near the entrance punctuates the house's geometric exterior; the shape is reiterated in the interior as a round dividing wall. The red door provides a splash of color.

Vallvidrera House

Location Vallvidrera, Spain **Photography** © Jordi Miralles

In this design, a building constructed at the beginning of the twentieth century was revamped into a new home for a young family of three. In order to maintain the relationship to the house's history, the architect decided to restore portions of the wall in the stair area instead of allowing them to disappear under a layer of plaster. By juxtaposing this brick structure with the iroko wood block staircase, the designer created a harmonious, energetic play of materials. In addition to its function, the staircase serves as an unobtrusive room divider that gives additional structure to the ground floor, separating the living area from the kitchen and dining areas. Furnishings and fittings developed specifically for this project include built-in kitchen cupboards that not only provide storage space, but also conceal the guest bath under the staircase. The warm colors of the wood in the living room contrast with the graphic, floral carpet in black, white, and red. By the same token, the bedrooms on the upper two levels were decorated in a fresh and natural manner yet contain sleek, minimalist furniture.

The furnishings and fittings were custom jobs by the interior designer, who planned the built-in kitchen cabinets that would not only provide storage space but also hide the guest bath.

The warm, natural iroko-wood cladding on the floors and cabinets contrasts with the central kitchen island made of stainless steel.

In order to maintain the relationship to the house's history, the architects decided to restore portions of the exisiting brick wall in the stair area instead of allowing them to disappear under a layer of plaster, as originally planned.

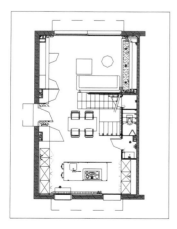

Ground floor

First floor

Second floor

The bedrooms on the upper two levels were decorated with natural materials in restrained colors such as white, beige, and blue to create an atmosphere both friendly and elegant.

Studio in Guadalajara

Location Guadalajara, Spain **Photography** © Luis Hevia

Used as a soap factory until the 1950's, this building has now been reborn as a house and workshop for the artist couple of Pedro Mora and Marta Sánchez-Bedoya. To maintain the original character of the building the designers decided to keep the vaulted ceilings and beams, and to use an existing recess as the kitchen entrance. Artworks, mostly by Mora, communicate the unique and eclectic character of the house; one example is a drawing of a female figure; that alludes to a video by the artist. The design is both creative and functional. The kitchen wall with a blackboard surface serves as a recipe repository as well as idea laboratory, (the notion is repeated in the workshop. A stairway of railroad ties leads up to the second floor, where the four bedrooms, bathroom, and dressing room are located. From the main bedroom, one can reach the top story, once the factory's drying furnace and now the location of a workshop.

Artworks, mostly created by Pedro Mora — such as the drawing of
a female figure, taken from a video by the artist—communicate the
house's unique and eclectic character.

To help sustain the original character of the building, the artist couple decided to use an existing recess as the kitchen entrance. The kitchen wall painted to serve as a blackboard functions as an idea laboratory as well.

The stairway of railroad ties leads to the second floor and directly into one of the four bedrooms. By its color, the orange wall adjacent to the stairway creates a visual link to the floor above.

The working areas, such as the office, were painted completely white to emphasize the lively and interesting artworks and materials.

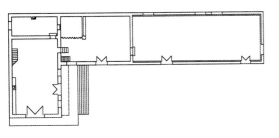

Ground floor

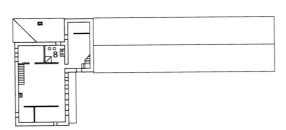

First floor

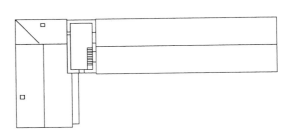

Second floor

On the top floor, once a drying furnace for the factory, the elements hanging from the ceiling evoke the room's history. The industrial atmosphere is set off by contemporary furnishings.

Hevia House

Location Sant Cugat del Vallès, Spain **Photography** © Luis Hevia

The footprint for this house in the center of the Catalonian city of Sant Cugat del Vallès is very narrow; as a result, the living area was built upwards, comprising six stories. Each floor has its own character due to its individual design and use of different materials. For example, because of its orange flooring causes, the lobby level to contrast with the next level, which is laid out in white stones. In the garage, a mezzanine level was designed, that can simultaneously be used as an office. Visually these two areas, which are very different in function, connect to one another by means of their shared yellow and orange tonality. A wooden staircase made of pinewood leads upstairs, to the children's room and bathroom. The bathroom walls were constructed in opaque synthetic material and bleached pinewood. This lively and humorous design is also manifested in the zebra-stripeed wooden floorboards and the pedestrian light which ensures the sink area is clear of traffic.

The top two floors were reserved for the public living areas: living room, dining room, kitchen, and terrace. To link these floors visually the connecting stairway was finished with metal bars extending throughout.

The humorous and lively design of the house is also evident in the kitchen, where one wall is a blackboard upon which the children can express themselves at their whim.

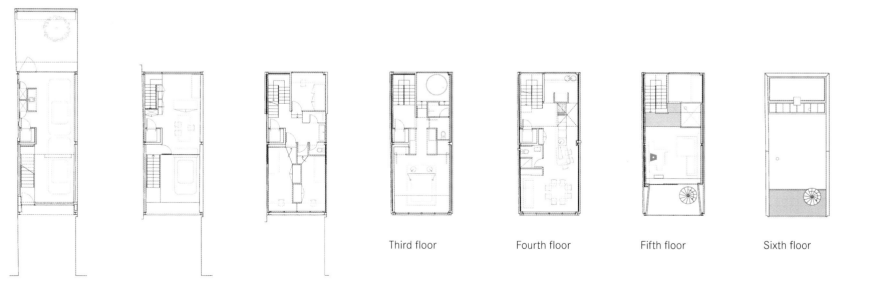

Ground floor

First floor

Second floor

Third floor

Fourth floor

Fifth floor

Sixth floor

The bathroom walls were constructed from an opaque synthetic material and bleached pinewood; a pedestrian light clears the crosswalk formed by the zebra-striped wooden floorboards.

House in Matadepera

Location Matadepera, Spain **Photography** © Nuria Fuentes

The focal point of this two-story single-family house is a fragmented wall that delineates the entrance area while also managing to integrate it with the living room and kitchen. This open partitioning and the absence of doors make the living room look much larger. The entrance area also benefits from big garden windows that provide ample sunlight, a crucial concern of architect Josep Mª Font of Greek. He combined natural lighting from the terrace window running along the entire front of the house with bands of light on the living room ceiling, illuminated niches in the dining room, and recessed bulbs in the kitchen. The color design helps emphasize the lighting concept; meanwhile, the foyer's asymmetric wall is highlighted by means of its blackness against the white interior walls. A splash of contrasting color and this basic palette is the red kitchen, which provides the design with depth and visual interest.

The living room receives abundant natural light from the large terrace window. Even so, the designer provided additional brightness via the light bands on the living room ceiling and the illuminated niches in the dining room.

The focal point of the ground floor is the interrupted black wall that separates the entrance area of the house from its living area and kitchen and provides striking visual contrast as well.

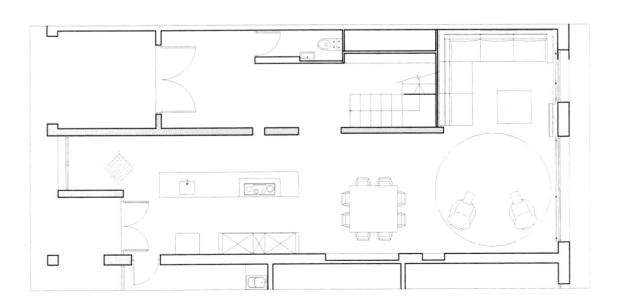

Plan

The monochromatic black-and-white palette is accentuated by
the kitchen's red wall and granite floors as well as by the wood
flooring in the bedroom.

Toorak House

Location Melbourne, Victoria, Australia **Photography** © Shania Shegedyn

This house is located in a shopping district on the outskirts of Melbourne. Since the lot is bordered on the left and right by single-story homes all along the property lines, a wall was added on the street side to create a large inner courtyard. Then the foyer of the house was shifted sideways towards the inner courtyard. From the entrance area, shaded by maple trees, one has a direct view of the inner courtyard and the living and dining areas through their sliding glass doors. With this open design, the multi-use rooms receive adequate light and a refreshing breeze. Light colors (accentuated with browns) also dominate the interiors. The polished concrete used indoors was extended to the pool from the living room, thereby reinforcing the connection between interior and exterior. From the stone garden, a stairway leads to the second story, where the bedrooms are located. They get ample natural light from the windows along the entire façade but retain privacy by means of a boundary wall.

From the entrance area, one can see the discreetly leafy inner courtyard, which provides the living and dining areas with natural light and fresh breezes.

To emphasize the airy, fresh atmosphere of the house, light colors and natural materials predominate in the interior design.

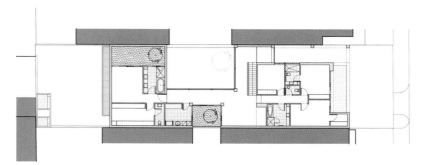

Ground floor

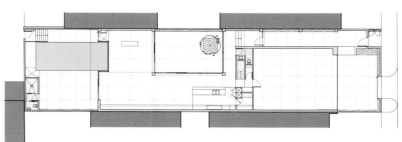

First floor

The bedrooms located on the second floor receive ample sunlight through the windows along the entire façade; at the same time, privacy is maintained thanks to the dividing wall of the property.

Zealandia House

Location Portsea, Victoria, Australia **Photography** © Shania Shegedyn

Located in Portsea, Australia, a beloved vacation spot for divers and surfers, this house was built in 1952. In designing its interiors, the architect thought it was important to give the house a modern look while also creating a link to its history by maintaining the aesthetics of the 1950s. For example, the original wooden kitchenette was maintained but updated with contemporary furniture and fittings. The bedroom's antique wall dressers were kept and renovated, while the bathrooms were completely revamped. The living room was also completely outfitted with new furniture. The modern decorative elements chosen by the architects were inspired by the style of the 1950s and often feature oval shapes and lively colors. An easygoing mix of wood, fabric, glass, stone, and leather in blue, gray, green, and beige tones creates a cozy yet summery atmosphere. Furthermore, the wood facing of the kitchenette is reiterated in the wooden-strip cladding on the living room wall. A splash of color is added to the white walls by the asymmetric stone fireplace. The adjacent sliding glass doors lead directly to the garden and seem to incorporate this green space into the living room as well.

The wood facing of the original kitchenette is reiterated in the wooden-strip wall cladding in the living room, which helps to create a fresh and cozy atmosphere in combination with the plank flooring and summery furnishings.

The living room was completely redesigned. The architects decided to use furnishings and decorative elements with oval shapes and dynamic colors that evoke the aesthetic of the 1950s.

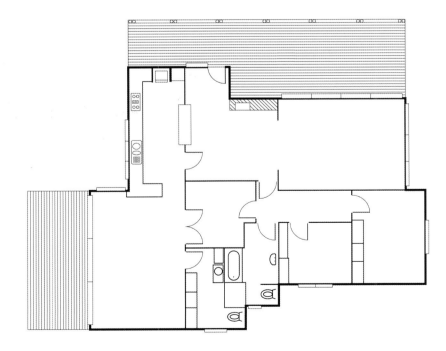

Plan

To help retain the original atmosphere of the house, antique wall armoires in the bedroom were kept and renovated. The bathroom, on the other hand, was completely redone with all the modern comforts.

NW3 Family House

Location Hampstead, UK **Photography** © Francesca Yorke

This single-family home was built at the beginning of the nineteenth century in the Edwardian style, and its new owners wanted an elegant and timeless design for the interiors. Like so many single-family homes in North London, it had been converted to an apartment house in the 1960s. To return it to its original function, the structure was partially changed, and from what had been the parlor and study, the architects created a spacious eat-in kitchen, which is connected to the living room. As a contrast to the granite-and-marble flooring of the kitchen, oak floors were installed in the new parlor. That room's built-in stainless-steel fireplace and cream-colored furnishings and fittings enhance the mood of relaxation. Furthermore, on the ground floor there is a spacious dining room, also in beige tones, with a black cast-iron fireplace and an antique candelabra from Capetown, South Africa. By means of the restored staircase (integrated into the room via staggered hanging lamps), one reaches the private rooms of the upper two floors. The eye-catcher of the master suite is the bathroom's "vanity island" with its luxurious chaise longue.

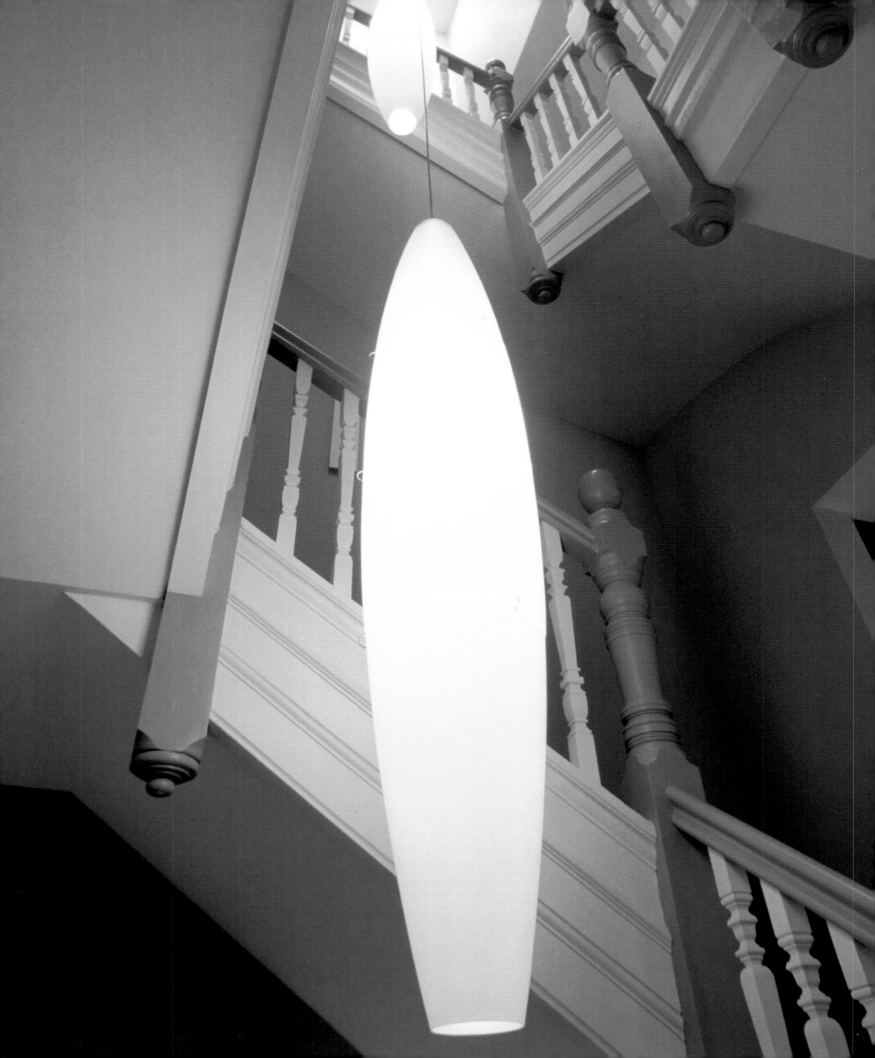

The future residents wanted an elegant and timeless design for the interiors; as part of that, the original stairway was restored, highlighted with the addition of stacked hanging lamps.

The eye-catcher of the discreet and luxurious master suite is the bathroom's "vanity island" with its luxurious chaise longue.

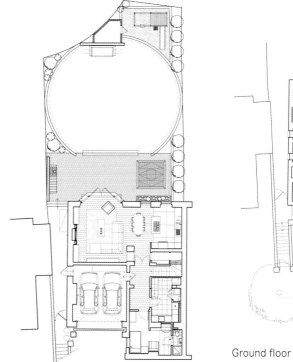

Lower ground floor

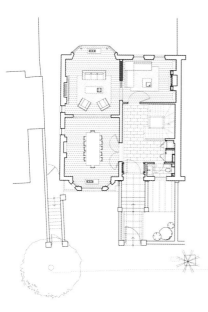

Ground floor

First floor

Second floor

Kelso House

Location Cremorne, Victoria, Australia **Photography** © Shania Shegedyn

In expanding this existing building in Cremorne's densely populated city center, the goal was to balance the need for natural light with the desired privacy. The architects resolved this issue by placing narrow glass bands in the roof and four glass doors in the façade bordering the garden. As a result, more sunlight can shine in but the living area is still unexposed to public view. The kitchen became the epicenter of the continuously designed house, as it connects the existing structure with the new extension. The section of the house now used as a study and living room was kept black to create an atmosphere that is simultaneously exciting and comfortable. The black flooring, coated in a shiny PURE varnish, is in harmony with the black bookshelves and curtain. As a contrast, the newly constructed dining area was painted white and its light concrete flooring was coated with a matte glaze. In this way, the different personalities of the individual living areas are maintained as the rooms also harmonize with one another.

A focal point of the open-plan house, the kitchen connects the existing study and living area with the new annex, enhancing the dynamic atmosphere.

With its matte glaze, the light concrete flooring of the dining area contrasts with the varnished black floors of the study and living room. However, both are furnished in black and white, which establishes a visual link between them.

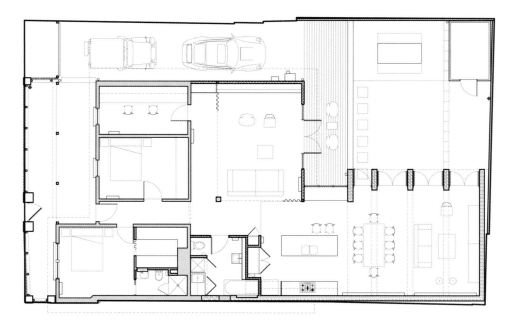

Plan

The black tiled bathroom receives natural light and interesting shadow play through the skylight. In keeping with this minimalist design, white installations and accessories were used.

The different characters of both the new and the already existin living spaces are furthermore reflected in the more private livin space. Therefore the bedroom — as a contrast to the dramati bathroom — is dominated by white colours.

F House in Mukonoso

Location Hyogo, Japan **Photography** © Mitsumasa Fujitsuka

This monochromatic design for a three-story single-family house emerged after the architect decided to surround the existing veranda with new walls. By means of this construction, the inner space of the cube, clad in steel plates, receives sufficient natural light. The dramatic effect of the black-and-white interiors is reinforced as irregular glass slots in the façade admit light that is reflected in laserlike stripes by the mirrorlike floor. The black porcelain, vinyl, and rubber tiles on the floor and staircase also contrast with the unplastered concrete walls. This reduced yet contrast-rich coloration is interrupted by shelf-like surfaces that zig-zag throughout the house to define the different areas. These not only serve as storage areas, benches, and balustrades, but also conceal installations like ventilation pipes and lighting cables. The house derives a unique character from this minimal design without comprimising function.

The asymmetric shelving that runs throughout the house on the two upper floors configures the kitchen (with its fold-out stove and sink) while concealing the necessary installation hardware.

The building, covered in zinc-clad steel plates incorporated an existing courtyard from which sunlight streams indoors.

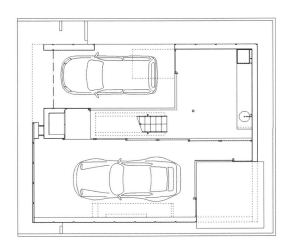

Ground floor

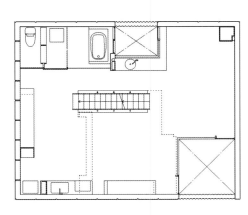

First floor

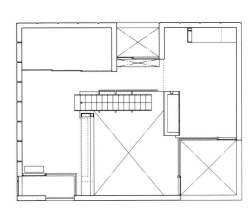

Second floor

The dramatic effect of the monochromatic interiors is reinforced
by the laserlike bands of light on the reflective flooring; the light
enters the house through irregular slits in the façade.

Lores House

Location Barcelona, Spain **Photography** © Jordi Miralles

A central element of this urban single-family house is the stairway finished in wenge wood; the communicative function of the staircase is further emphasized by glass cladding. The pleasant coffee-colored tonality of the wenge wood was also used in the flooring, which helps to create an elegant, unified, and comfortable environment, in an array of brown tones. These also appear in the furnishings – chairs, dining table, carpets, and the headboard of the bed. The wall surfaces, made of white and beige marble and gypsum, blend well with the shades of brown. The dining and living rooms are located on the ground floor. They flow into each other, but can be separated as needed. From both rooms, one has views of the pool in the garden and the roofed terrace. This area also features white marble and wood, and is surrounded by olive trees, carob trees, and palm trees typical of the region. The more private rooms are located on the upper floors. On those levels, sliding doors provide a flexible and consequently more spacious layout, which is emphasized by light beige and brown tones.

The combination of marble- and gypsum-clad walls and furnishin[g] in various brown tones make the dining and living areas ir[] comfortable environments. They can be opened up to create o[] large space, or separated into two, as needed.

Ground floor

First floor

Second floor

The more private rooms are located on the upper floors. Sliding doors provide a flexible layout, the spaciousness of which is emphasized by light beige and brown tones.

The garden with a pool and the roofed terrace were designed to feature white marble and wood, and are surrounded by olive trees, carob trees, and palm trees typical of the region.

LOFTS

Loft Schorndorf

Location Schorndorf, Stuttgart, Germany **Photography** © Zooey Braun

For a long time, gabled roofs were a mark of conservative architecture. However, this conversion of a factory building into a loft demonstrates that gabled roofs can be an inventive, successful, and visually appealing way to create additional living space. The 150-square-meter addition to the loft was divided into two levels for optimal use of the space. By placing the bathroom and bedroom on the upper floor, the architect ensured sufficient privacy without the need for disruptive dividing walls. The lower level, which comprises the living room and kitchen, centers on a zebrano wood–clad box, which also joins both living levels vertically with one another and creates space for a small bathroom. An unobtrusive steel stairway leads to the upper mezzanine. Here the open design of the lower floor enables those upstairs to enjoy the view from the large window through the glass balustrade. The bathroom projects into the space and is separated visually from the surrounding yarra wood flooring by a slightly raised Crema Baida natural stone floor. Such stylish mixtures of different materials give the loft an intimate feeling despite its size.

The zebrano wood-clad box and the reddish yarra wood parquet flooring enrich the open, white loft by creating a pleasant, natural aspect.

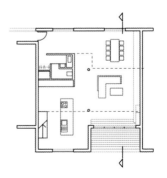

Ground floor

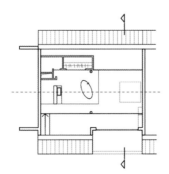

First floor

Section

The bathroom projects into the open space and is visually set off from the rest by its slightly raised Crema Baida natural stone flooring amid the yarra wood parquet.

Duplex Sarrià Samsó

Location Barcelona, Spain **Photography** © Jordi Miralles

This two-story loft is located in a five-story apartment building in Sarrià, one of the most elegant neighborhoods in Barcelona. At the center of this tasteful design is the U-shaped living area where floors, walls, and ceiling are clad in wood, and yellow and orange Egg chairs provide colorful accents. It is separated visually from the kitchen area by a gray couch. Another interesting detail is the installation of the flatscreen TV. Instead of hanging it from the ceiling, as is customary, or placing it on a table, the designer fastened it to the ceiling by means of a pivot-mounted arm; it can thus be positioned to face any corner. Like the living area, the kitchen was clad in wood panels on the ceiling and cabinet fronts but was refreshed with a stainless-steel work surface. The adjacent eating area blends well with this thanks to its inviting leather chairs. Cones of light from the white ceiling lamp also helps to define this area. A wooden staircase then leads to the bedroom situated within a glassed-in mezzanine. In harmony with the overall concept, the ceiling, floor, and sections of the walls there were clad in wood as well.

The warm tones of the wood paneling and flooring in the living and dining areas, complimented by the gray living room sofa and the graphic gray and black carpeting, create a cozy yet refreshing atmosphere.

The wood-clad kitchen was freshened up by the stainless-steel
work surface and appliances.

Ground floor

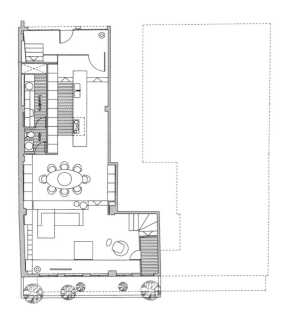

First floor

A wooden stairway leads to the glassed-in mezzanine. Staggered oval ceiling lights contrast with the sharp rectangular contours of the structure and compensate for lack of natural lighting.

The bathroom's beige marble lining creates a comfortable atmosphere, yet it has a very elegant look. In addition, the halogen spot
lighting of the bathroom cabinet accentuates the shelves and
enhances the simplicity of the design.

The bedroom was clad almost entirely in wood. The stair-shaped
bed frame, which also serves as a bench and night table, is unique.

Loft Granollers

Location Granollers, Barcelona, Spain **Photography** © Gogortza & Llorella

This loft is a part of a project in which the second floor of an industrial building was converted into two similar, yet differently decorated, lofts. The industrial appearance of the space was to be maintained, so the exisitng ventilation and lighting systems were integrated into the new concept. The oblong space is structured around an inserted box in its center. In addition to containing a bathroom, it serves as a room divider separating the sleeping area from the living area. To emphasize this separation, the cube was painted red on all sides except the one facing the kitchen; this differentiates it from the elements of the living area, which are mostly ochre, orange, and beige. These color tones give the cool, industrial loft setting a warm and sunny feeling. The kitchen also combines these two contrary ideas: the work surfaces were finished in stainless steel, a contrast to the light wood cladding of the kitchen cupboards. And the industrial character of the original aluminum window panes is softened by white curtains that extend down to the floor and gently filter the sunlight.

The living area was outfitted in ochre, orange and beige to give the cool, industrial loft a warm and sunny feeling.

The wooden panelling of the kitchen cupboards was chosen in order to bring a warm and sunny ambience into the rather cool and industrial atmosphere of this loft. At the same time, the industrial character is echoed in the stainless steel worktop.

The bathroom is inside a box structure in the center of the loft; the red cube serves as a clothes closet and as a room divider, and its color visually separates the sleeping area from the living area.

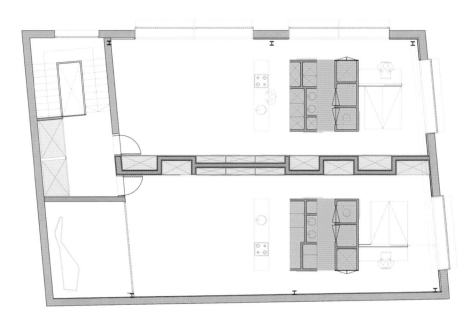

Plan

Alejandra Fierro Loft

PILAR | LÍBANO

Location Barcelona, Spain **Photography** © Gogortza & Llorella

This loft comprises a four-room apartment in which rooms fulfilling various functions are grouped around the kitchen, the focal point of the space. Integrating the closets and drawers into the wall cladding helps to create an organized and spacious atmosphere in this relatively small loft, where one discovers the individual functions bit by bit. For this sleek and effective solution, furnishings and fittings were personally designed and custom-finished by the architect, Pilar Líbano. Behind a seamlessly installed door is a well-concealed bathroom made of white marble, and elsewhere sliding doors divide or unify rooms for multiple uses of the space. Mostly white and sand-colored tones give the loft a minimalist, sunny feel, assisted by the oak flooring. Striking, colorful wall drawings of a microphone in the kitchen and a large palm tree in the stairwell add whimsy; transparent cladding on the spiral staircase opens up the view of the palm drawing to underscore the loft's distinctive character.

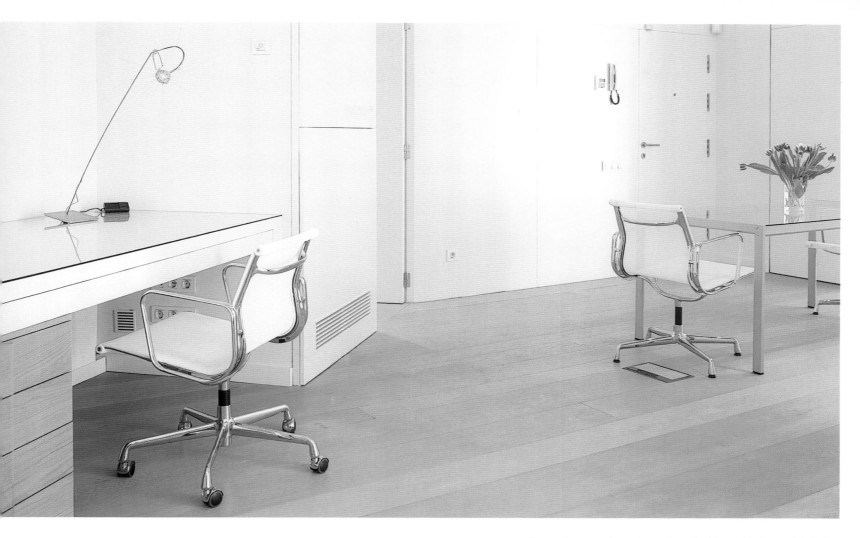

To create a spacious atmosphere in this relatively small loft, the wall claddings incorporate closets, drawers, and doors; only upon closer inspection does one discover the white marble bathroom behind this closed door.

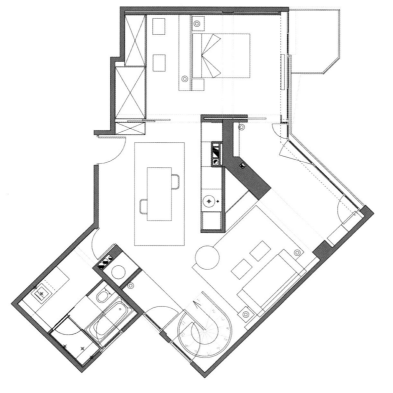

Plan

The kitchen is the focal point of the loft; it can be closed off by a sliding door as needed. The cheerful character of the space is exemplified by a colorful drawing of a microphone.

The minimalist design of the furnishings and fittings are set off by
the organic look of the oak flooring. Ingo Maurer lamps provide
sufficient light along with light bands on the ceiling.

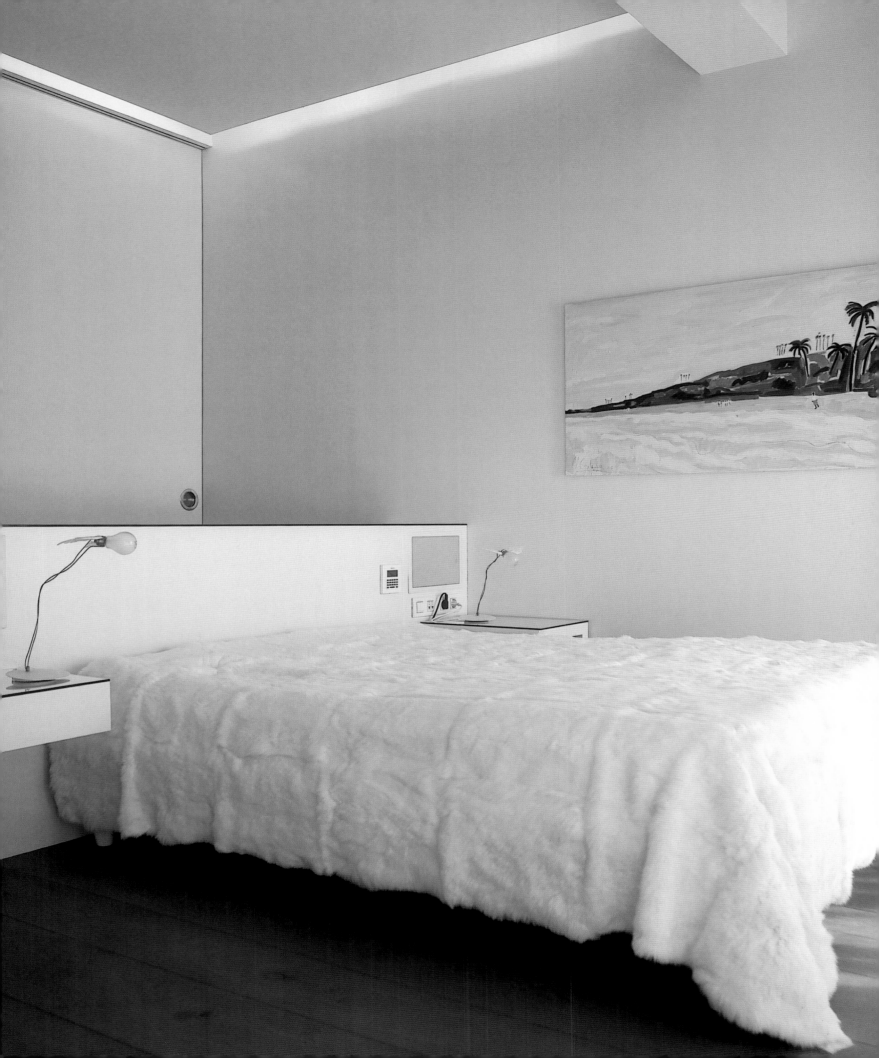

Park Avenue Loft

Location New York, USA   **Photography** © Åke E:son Lindman

The space for this Park Avenue loft came out of the merger of two apartments. The three bedrooms, bathroom, guest room, living and dining areas were arranged in an open, L-shaped floor plan. The wet area (kitchen and bath) is in the center of the loft, with the bedroom on one side and the living area on the other. Dividing walls were intentionally omitted; an amorphous partition separates the parlor from the dining room. This partition not only adds coziness, but also showcases the unique lighting design. Directly above the dining table and sofa, three recessed light wells were installed to help create a warm yet striking look. The floating effect of the partition's built-in, lower ceiling is intensified by the lighting of the intervening space. The living areas run perpendicular to the sleek bedrooms, which also feature gray and white tones. The reduced color palette is accented by orange and yellow elements to enhance the minimalist flair of the loft.

The kitchen can be separated from the dining room by means of a translucent glass-and-steel-sliding door. The kitchen also has its own eating area independent of the dining room.

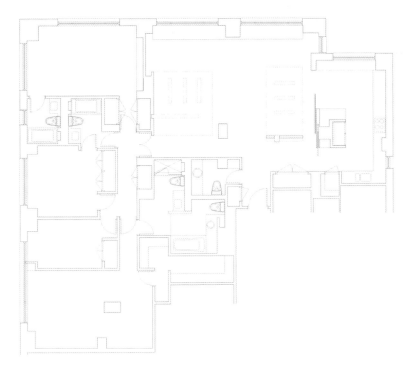

Plan

The sleek bedroom's gray and white tones are accented by decorative elements in orange and yellow to enrich the minimalist flair.

Porthole Loft

DESAI CHIA | ARCHITECTURE

Location New York, USA **Photography** © Paul Warchol

In the conversion of this industrial loft for a young family, the challenge was to unite two seemingly contrary concepts. The open character of the loft was to be maintained, but areas that could be separated were needed to guarantee the required privacy. As a result, the three bedrooms were configured by means of translucent doors, and the bathroom, at the center of the loft, was set off from the living room inside a box of ash wood panels. Stainless-steel openings at regular intervals in the panels of the box allow daylight to reach the interior; balloon-shaped ceiling lamps complement this attractive lighting design. The light-flooded look of this open environment is supported by the color palette which has been reduced to white, gray and beige. The gray of the floor in the living area is repeated in the sofa and table and is simultaneously contrasted with the orange and black chairs as well as the graphic black-and-white sofa. As an additional splash of color, the paneled storage space of the bedroom dividing wall was also colored orange, thereby reinforcing the connection to the entrance area.

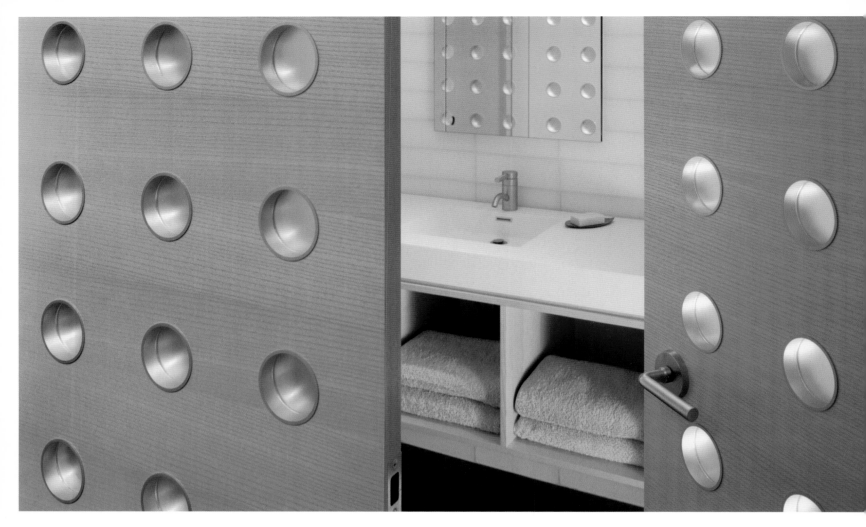

The bathroom was isolated at the center of the loft inside a box of ash tree panels. Stainless-steel openings in the panels at regular intervals create interesting reflections.

Opaque doors separate the three bedrooms from the main livin space thus preserving the open character of the loft yet guara teeing privacy when required.

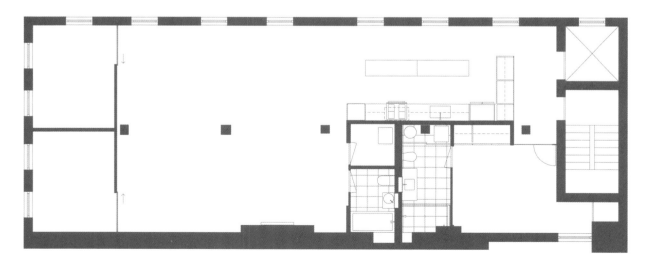

Plan

Chameleon Warehouse Extension

Location Melbourne, Victoria, Australia **Photography** © John Gollings

In this spacious converted Melbourne candy factory, the central element is its red crystal structure. Inspired by a ship's hull, this enormous glass sculpture configures the open, high-ceilinged space. A staircase leads to the deck and directly to the bedroom, which has a very cozy feeling thanks to the red walls and floor. To complement the intense color of this relatively small space, one wall was clad almost entirely in mirrors. Those mirrors, in conjunction with the windows and the box-shaped lamps directly above the bed, help spread light through the room. The red tonality of the crystal structure is echoed in the original red brick on the rear wall of the loft. The kitchenette here receives ample natural light from two large windows. The bathroom also has an open design and was set up within a recess in the imposing red glass structure; its interesting light and color elements are reflected via asymmetrically mounted mirrors.

The red tonality of the crystal sculpture is in harmony with the original brick wall in the kitchen, which features two large windows.

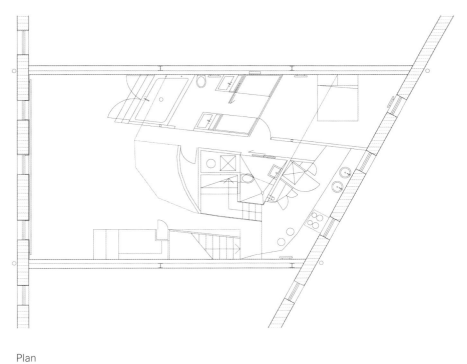

Plan

The bathroom was configured within a niche in the imposing
glass body; interesting light and color reflections appear in
asymmetrically positioned mirrors.

Loft for Video Artists

Location London, UK **Photography** © Peter Guenzel

Like those of other architects, the designs of Plasma Studio's London-based designers, Eva Castro and Holger Kehne, are drawn on a computer. Unlike with other projects, however, the renderings perfectly match the final result. This conversion of a once industrial building for two video artists succeeds because the volumes comprising the living and working areas were perfectly calculated. To avoid restricting the expansive space with walls, the designers decided on a minimalist, open layout in which the various areas are defined by transparent sliding doors and sculptural furnishings. However, because of the artists' work with video screens, the designers wanted to keep the interiors rather dark. The unusual appearance of the fixtures and fittings is reinforced by means of built-in neon lamps which only partially illuminate the space and make the furnishings seem to float in the air. The glimmering effect is enhanced by the of white, shiny wood floors. In contrast to this polished environment, the bath retains the original, rustic masonry and features a wooden bathtub.

In order to create a minimalist, open layout, the designers defined individual functional areas by transparent sliding doors and sculptural furnishings.

bathroom

darkroom

bedroom

living room

kitchen

office

Plan

The clear and reflective atmosphere elsewhere in the loft contrasts with
the design of the bath, in which the original brickwork with its defects was
preserved and a wooden bathtub was installed.

Ray 1

Location Vienna, Austria **Photography** © Rupert Steiner

One can close the gap between two gables in many ways, but rarely, does one encounter such a bold example of the term *roof landscape*. An office building from the 1960s serves as a foundation for the new home of the Delugan Meissl family of architects. By means of folds and recesses, a residential landscape was then worked out in which the interior design is subordinated to the overall concept. Visibility and flexibility are minimized and most of the furnishings are firmly anchored. This begins in the foyer in which the wall contains an invisible closet and doors on rollers disappear into the

walls. Switches and plugs were kept to a minimum: Light switches, sometimes penny-sized, sit in steel plates. Even the bed floats immovable in the bedroom. Both bathrooms are designer masterpieces in their own right. The parents' bath, for example, takes the form of a monolithic, snow-white synthetic block incorporating tub, basin, sunken light bands, and screens lit from behind. Here too, the architects renounced handles—everything opens with the gentle touch of a hand.

Folds and recesses define this crystalline living area where the fittings are anchored strongly in the room.

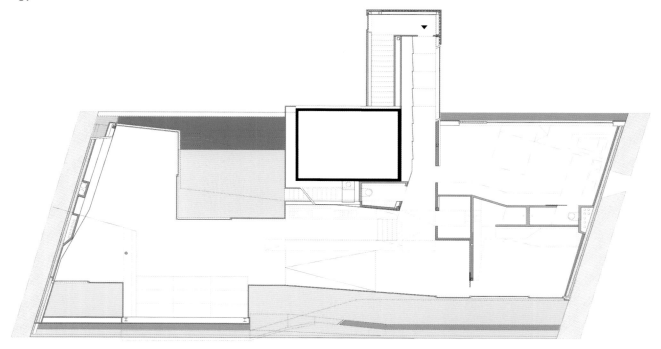

Plan

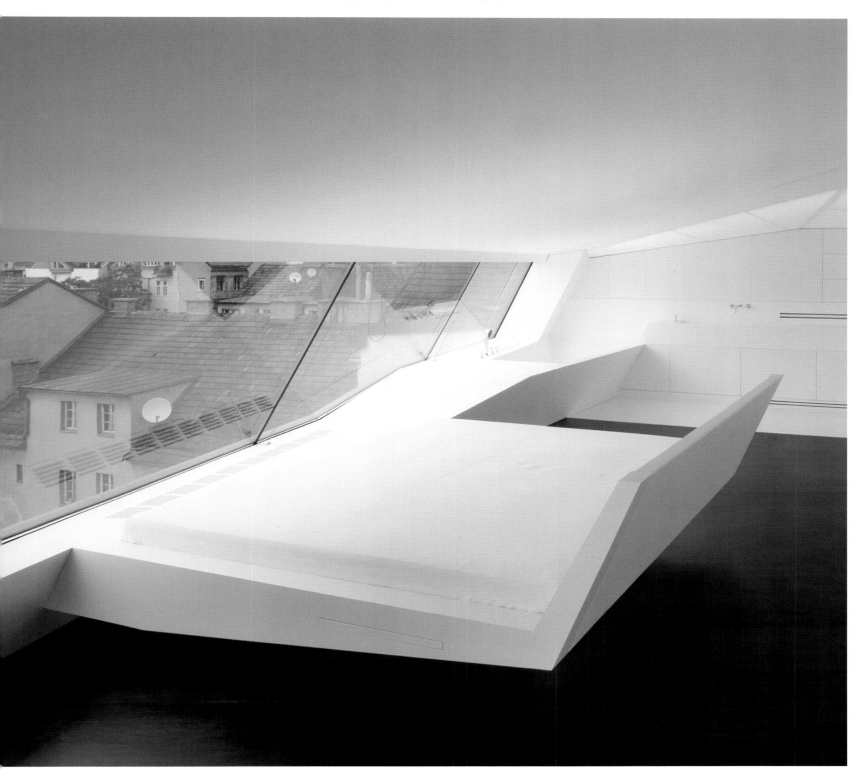

his living space was created through cuts and convolutions and
xtends even until the roof terrace that can be reached via a ramp.
he large glass windows further enhance the harmonic blending
etween inside and outside.

Switches, connectors, furnishings, fittings, and other details
were reduced to a minimum so as to accord with the futuristic
atmosphere; even the bed floats immovably in the space.

The bathroom—an integrated masterpiece in itself—is configured within a monolithic, snow-white synthetic block that includes tub, basin, sunken light bands, and screens lit from behind.

Storefront Loft

Location New York, USA **Photography** © Elizabeth Felicella

A street-level loft in New York City's East Village is the current design project of architects Brian Messana and Toby O'Rorke. The future residents wanted not only a comfortable home but also a showroom space for their contemporary art and furniture collection. To achieve this, the original 12-foot ceiling height was maintained and a continuous white coat of paint creates a neutral background interrupted only by the black lacquered floor and the restored steel columns and wood beams. To sustain the airy impression and to direct attention to the decorative elements—table, sofa and chaise longue—the architects concealed the required storage space. A window slit on the southern side of the living room facing the street provides the desired sunlight: Its view of the sky is combined with a 50-foot-long light strip, where individual spots create islands of light. The orthogonally appointed kitchen fits into this monochromatic loft thanks to its white lacquered surfaces and the stainless-steel cladding of the work area, a combination that accords with this sleek, yet by no means colorless, environment.

A window slit on the southern end of the living room, facing the street, provides the desired natural lighting. This view of the sky is combined with a 50-foot-long light strip where individual spots act as accents.

The orthogonally appointed kitchen harmonizes with the monochromatic loft thanks to the combination of white lacquered surfaces with the stainless-steel cladding of the work area.

The future residents were seeking to showcase their contemporary
art and furniture collection in the apartment, so the walls were
painted white to create a neutral backdrop.

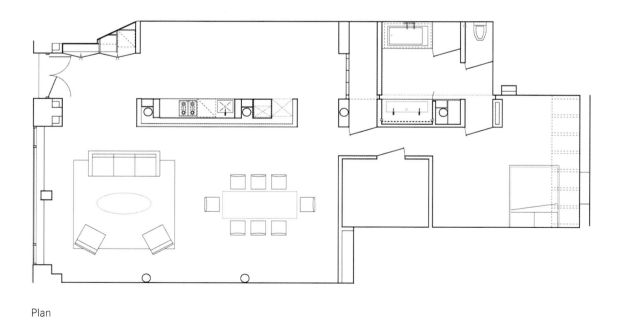

Plan

Morgan Residence

Location New York, USA **Photography** © Björg Magnea

This loft in Greenwich Village was created during the conversion of a commercial building. In order to keep its industrial character while modernizing it at the same time, the architects had the brick ceiling restored and the white-oak floor bleached. The loft derives its contemporary character from the sleek, white built-in closets, which serve as both room dividers and furnishings. Where the upper portions of the wall plates were left out, the lower half serves as a bench and shelf. The headboard of the bed was also integrated into the walk-in closet, with a covered light row enhancing the built-in look. The loft receives natural light from the window in the parlor and a sliding glass door next to the kitchen, but this light is insufficient. To compensate, architects Jason Tang and Maki Kawasaki placed ample light balloons around the loft, especially in the kitchen area and bedroom. These points of light were augmented by indirect light strips in the kitchen work space and in the seating corner to provide full illumination of this sleek environment.

To maintain the loft's industrial character, the brick ceiling was restored and paired with sleek, white built-in closets that give the apartment a contemporary feel.

Plan

The white MDF plate-finished module configures the storage space of the loft. Parts of this module were omitted and the resulting space was designed to serve as a bench seat, highlighted by a concealed light strip.

Loft in the Born

Location Barcelona, Spain **Photography** © Gogortza & Llorella

In this project, the architect, Ignasi Pérez, and the interior designer, Cristina Fernandez, converted an apartment in a landmark building into a loft. In the process, they had to tailor their design concept to adhere to landmark-protection regulations. The rules required keeping the ceiling beams, window shutters, and the terrace, and excluded the option of illuminating the somewhat dark surroundings by expanding the window or by building in an areaway. As a result, the designers created an open and seamless environment in which a curving counter unites the rooms: It is a work area for the kitchen that can also be used as a dining table. The stove and refrigerator are encased in an orange unit, which serves as a room divider, but because it does not reach the ceiling, will also admit the light from the living room windows to enter the interior. In addition to its function as an armoire, it also acts as a visual shield for the bed behind it. The bathroom, arranged sideways, is visible from the sleep area and defined by its pistachio-green boundary wall.

The work space of the kitchen, which can also be used as a dining table, extends into the living room, thereby creating a visual connection between the two areas.

In addition to its actual function as a clothes closet, the added orange structure serves to shield the bed to the rear. The walls were designed not to extend all the way to the ceiling in order to admit natural light indoors.

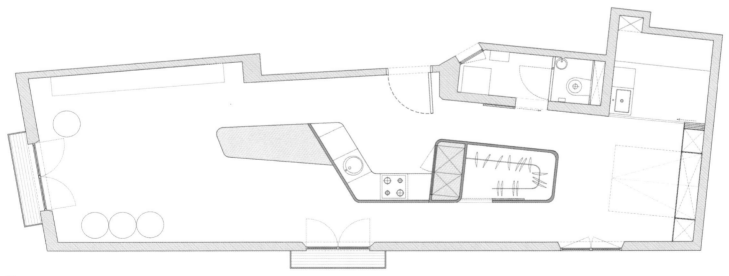

Plan

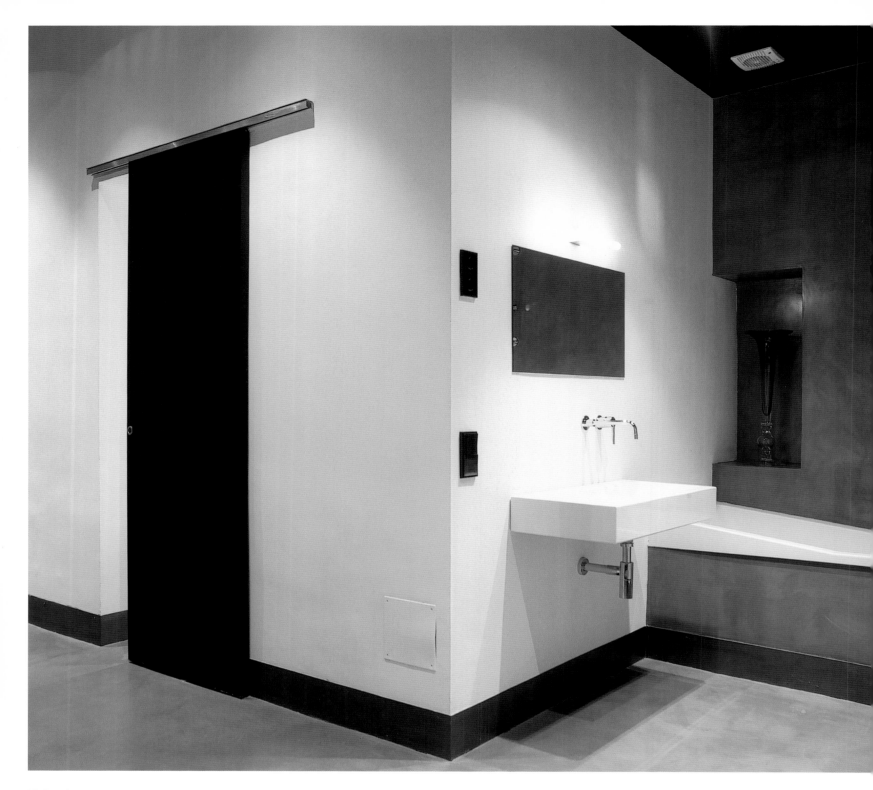

Visible from the sleeping area, the bathroom was arranged in an open layout. Only the toilet was concealed. The white porcelain sink and Norman Foster bathtub contrast with the black hand-towel dryer and the pistachio-green paint on one wall.

Loft Pere IV

JOSEP CANO | I DAMUNT

Location Barcelona, Spain **Photography** © Gogortza & Llorella

The original structure of this two-story loft was built at the beginning of the nineteenth century. The 1936-square-foot area comprises a long, rectangular room, which is complemented by a patio on the lower level and a terrace above. The top priority for the design was to keep the existing structure. This is why the brick walls and ceiling arches were not covered—instead, they were restored and integrated into the overall design concept. Natural materials were also used for the parquet floor (birchwood) and the custom-made armoires (cherry wood), in contrast to the sleek, contemporary furnishings. One reaches the somewhat smaller second floor by means of an iron stairway with wooden steps. This stair was placed next to the wall so as not to obstruct the free space between the two floors: keeping the space open was crucial because, except for the opaque entrance door and a terrace at the end of the lower level, there are no windows. Natural light enters by means of a translucent sliding door that divides the library and the office on the top floor. As in an atrium, sunlight filters into the interior.

The top priority for the design was to keep the existing structure. This is why the brick walls were not covered but restored instead; they are in contrast to contemporary, sleek furnishings.

One reaches the somewhat smaller second floor by means of an iron stairway with wooden steps. Thanks to its placement against the wall, the existing areaway is not obstructed, which allows sunlight to stream.

To create a comfortable atmosphere in the bedroom, natural materials were used, such as birch wood for the flooring and cherry wood for the built-in closets, all combined with a reddish brick wall.

Loft B-3

Location Barcelona, Spain **Photography** © Jordi Miralles

In this former industrial building, portions of the original structure, such as water pipes, aluminum ventilation pipes, and iron girders, were maintained and integrated into the renovation design. To create a homier feeling given the imposing ceiling height, a mezzanine was constructed and the living space distributed over two levels. At the same time, the ceiling was painted dark gray and the walls painted light gray to reinforce this effect visually. The color gray, in its various shades, also dominates the furnishings— for example, the iron dining table and the matching stools by Ermeco. This minimalist color palette is brightened up by the orange bookcase, designed by the architect, that serves as a room divider between the work area and dining table. The kitchen is a special attraction. It can be hidden by sliding doors as needed, thereby revealing a book shelf. On the top level, the gray stone floor of the lower level is supplanted by a wood parquet floor. This creates a warmer atmosphere in the bedroom and bathroom there and fits harmoniously within the overall industrial concept.

In the furnishings, the color gray dominates on various levels. This reduced color palette is livened up by the orange shelving, devised by the interior designer; the bookcase also serves as a room divider between the office and dining table.

The orange shelf designed by the architect functions as a room divider. In addition, it forms a contrast to the grey coloured walls, the iron dining table as well as the matching chairs.

The kitchen is a special attraction. It can be covered by slidin doors when desired, thereby revealing integrated book shelve transforming the table area into a type of library.

The bedroom closets were made of translucent panels, which allow light from the side windows to pass through unobstructed.

Instead of the gray stone flooring of the lower level, wooden floors were installed to help create a warm atmosphere in the bedroom and bathroom.

APARTMENTS

Penthouse

Location Zaragoza, Spain **Photography** © Jordi Miralles

In the conversion of this attic-floor apartment, the design challenge was the various ceiling heights, an issue resolved by means of a well-thought-out open design incorporating the use of light colors. In the lowest and most inclined wall, three window slits produce an interesting lighting effect. The designer decided to reserve this area for the sofa, an attention-grabbing orange Zanotta couch that was combined with a stainless-steel coffee table and original chairs custom-made for this project. A Le Corbusier chaise longue,

which the client had purchased in a Danish antiques shop, was added, too. This open layout was repeated in the bedroom, which is separated from the living area by only a crystal wall. The discreet bathroom was enlivened by a peppy wall painting. Because the ceiling was especially high near the entrance, the designer decided to build an intermediate floor there and to use the added space as a guest room. Yet another intermediate floor is located in the kitchen area. It can be reached by climbing an electric fold-out ladder.

In the lowest and most inclined wall, three window slits provide an interesting lighting effect. This is why the designer decided to reserve this area for the sofa and the Le Corbusier chaise longue.

To create additional storage space in the kitchen area, the designer installed a mezzanine which can be reached by means of an electric fold-out ladder.

In this open-plan layout, the seperate bathroom is concealed behind a tinted glass sliding door. A peppy wall painting catches the eye in this neutral white environment.

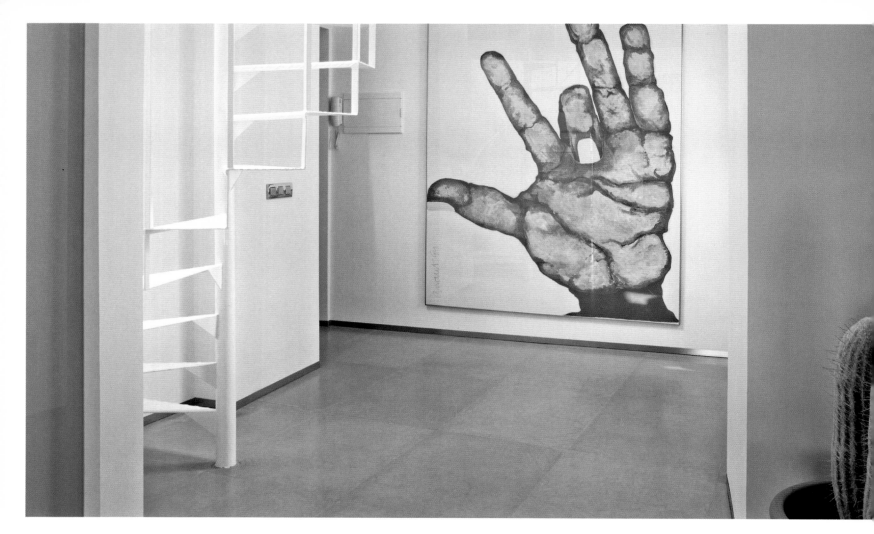

The ceiling was especially high near the entrance, so the designer decided to install a mezzanine floor here, gaining space to use as a guest room. A spiral staircase next to the bathroom leads directly to the new addition.

Plan

Xabi Riba Apartment

Location Barcelona, Spain **Photography** © Gogortza & Llorella

The main objective of this design was to make better use of the living area. Consequently, unnecessary dividing walls were removed and replaced with sliding doors to create a more flexible layout. The kitchen and foyer thereby merged; that space was completely clad in oak wood, which was also used for the flooring. The cane chairs of the dining area also emphasize the warm and natural ambience. Additional living space was also created by incorporating the terrace into the living room. However, the separate status of this sunny addition is underscored by covering its floor in a light brown loop-pile carpet instead of wooden tiles. The large windows of the balcony also illuminate the adjacent living room from all sides. Warm tones (such as white and beige) and natural materials (such as linen and velvet) provide a cozy feeling in which the furnishings play a major role. In keeping with the basic concept of openness, the bedrooms and bathroom are separated from one another only by glass panels. At the same time, privacy is preserved since the bathroom is entered via its own sliding door.

The kitchen and entrance area were completely clad in the oak panels also used for the flooring. Along with the cane chairs of the dining area, the wood creates a warm and natural atmosphere.

To optimize the use of space, unnecessary dividing walls were replaced by sliding doors. In a nod to this basic concept, the bedrooms and bathroom were separated from one another only by glass panels.

The terrace was enclosed and incorporated into the existing living area. This peaceful oasis maintains its separateness, however, via floors clad in light brown sisal carpeting instead of wooden tiles.

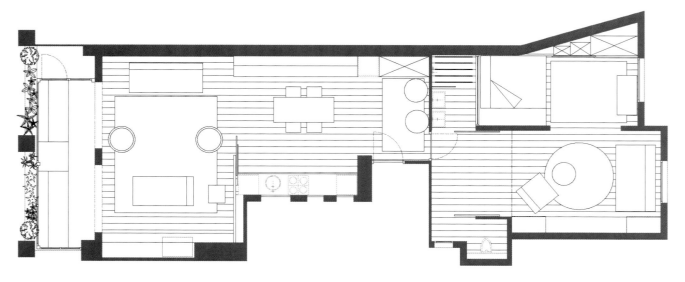

Plan

Boters Street Residence

Location Barcelona, Spain **Photography** © Nuria Fuentes

For this 387-square-foot apartment in the historic center of Barcelona, the objective was to plan the limited space so that a couple could live there comfortably. The architects solved this challenging problem in a practical and attractive way. Using MDF plates suspended from tracks in the ceiling, they created dynamic room dividers, which can be combined in ever-changing ways. The white lacquered wall screens were broken up by irregular circular perforations, so they can also be used to filter the light coming in from the balcony door. Halogen ceiling lamps complement this simple yet efficient lighting system. Moreover, the architects concentrated on a reduced but contrast-rich color palette. The floor was covered in black tiles; the white walls visually expand the restricted space. Splashes of color are found in the orange kitchen. It's dining table also serves as a work table; it can be pushed backward and forward on its large casters.

To visually expand the small space, the walls and ceiling were
painted white in contrast to the black flooring. The dining table,
built on casters, also serves as a movable partition.

The MDF-plate room dividers running on tracks around the ceiling are perforated by irregularly positioned circles; as a result, the screens can be used to filter light coming in from the balcony door.

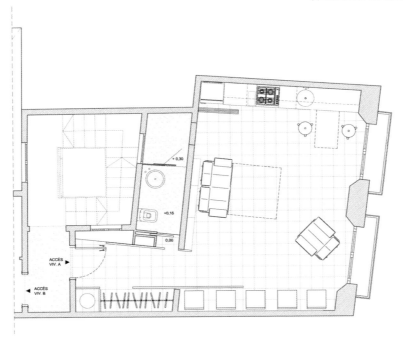

Plan

Apartment Enric Rovira

Location Barcelona, Spain **Photography** © Gogortza & Llorella

Renowned Spanish chocolate artist Enric Rovira wanted an apartment that would also incorporate an office and showroom as an extension of his shop downstairs. At the same time, the work and living areas had to be clearly separate, so the entrance was used to divide the apartment in half visually. The living area is on the left and the work area is on the right. The office was defined by placing a large, white worktable in the center; the showroom, created from a storage space, was especially designed to accommodate the various chocolate package sizes, and features a built-in projector that displays images on the wall near white leather chairs that invite the viewer to take a seat. Owing to skillful details like the completely equipped yet discreetly integrated kitchen, the interior design has a futuristic look, reinforced by the monochromatic color palette. This reduced tonality does not seem cold, however, thanks to the warm oak flooring. The bed is unique: Its frame contains storage space and the sleeping area can be closed off by means of a sliding tinted glass pane, evoking a space capsule.

A large, white worktable along with a projection area and a storage space especially designed for the various candy package sizes add up to a complete office with showroom despite the limited square footage.

The client wanted a clear separation between his work area and living area, so the architect, Francesc Rifé, decided to use the entrance as a room divider; by doing so, he would not have to sacrifice space for building walls.

As part of the minimalist, high-tech aesthetic, the kitchen is
complete yet discreetly concealed; its oak table and flooring
add a bit of warmth.

Due to the limited space, a separate TV room was not created; the television sits just inside the bedroom on a built-in night table.

The bed is unique in design. It is set in a niche that can be closed off like a space capsule behind a sliding tinted glass pane. Around the bed, geometrically shaped cladding was used to create additional storage space.

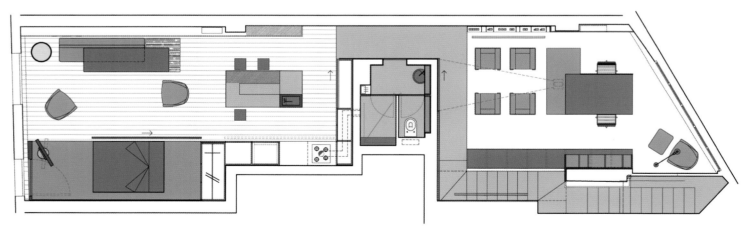

Plan

A3-3 Apartment

Location Eindhoven, Netherlands **Photography** © Peter Cuypers

This spacious, open living area was created from the conversion of a historic building. The 2,100-square-foot, all-encompassing living room occupies two levels, while to accord with this airy design, the upper floor was designed as a mezzanine. A narrow corridor leads to the master bedroom, children's room, and the bathroom, and provides a view of the open television room on the lower floor. In another section of that room is an elevated platform where black furniture invites relaxation. A gap between these two areas leads to the kitchen and dining room. A five-foot-wide aquarium situated in one wall serves as a visual connector between the kitchen and the TV room (and is also partially visible from the bathroom); in addition, it helps enrich the white walls. In the white dining room, a fireplace in the wall and an illuminated rectangular ceiling vault provide a festive ambience. This monochromatic color palette enhances the apartment's feeling of spaciousness, as do such details as the transparent open stairway.

The monochromatic color palette of this design delineates the space. For example, the relaxation areas are emphasized by their black furnishings, which contrast with the white dining room.

The kitchen and TV room are located next to one another, divided by a separating wall that contains a five-foot-long aquarium. Not only is the fish tank a special eye-catcher, but it is also a unifying element in the décor.

The open and spacious design of the apartment is underscored by such details as the transparent, open crystal stairway that leads to the upper floor.

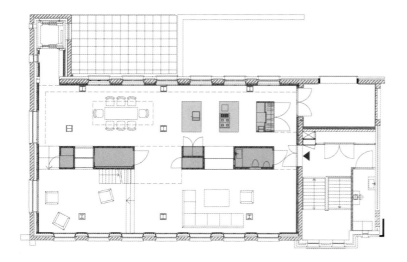

Ground floor

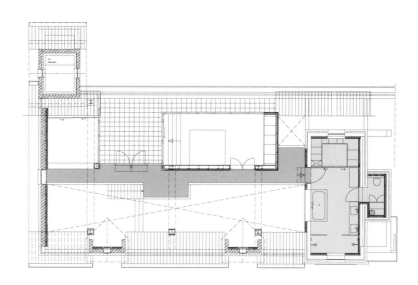

First floor

On the upper level, a mezzanine, a long narrow corridor leads to the bedrooms and bathroom. The slant of the roof was emphasized here by means of the black-and-white contrast.

Laura House

Location Rome, Italy **Photography** © Luigi Filetici

This apartment for a young career woman in Rome captivates the visitor because of its unusual configuration. The glassed-in shower, its floor piled with pebbles, is located next to the half-height kitchenette, from which one has a direct view of the living and dining areas' furnishings and fittings, custom-designed for this project. Configured in an L shape, this section is separated from the adjacent foyer by an opaque glass pane. The open-plan apartment also uses sliding doors of dark oak wood, which separate the office from the kitchen and shower area as needed. From the office, one proceeds to the bedroom, where white lacquered closets provide a refreshing note and the lighting design plays a major role, as it does elsewhere in the apartment. Halogen-light accents are combined with fluorescent light strips, especially in the room's angles. This intense lighting design is reinforced by the white tonality of the walls and furnishings.

Its lighting design and unusual layout make this open-plan apartment appealing. The glassed-in shower, its floor is piled with pebbles, is located right next to the half-height kitchenette.

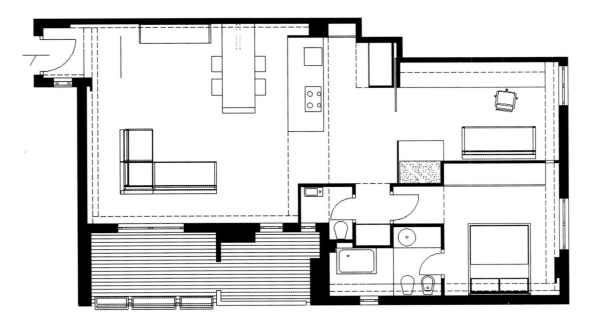

Plan

To emphasize the airy design, the white paint was combined with a lighting scheme that includes fluorescent light strips, especially in the corners.

Apartment Igualada

Location Igualada, Barcelona, Spain **Photography** © Gogortza & Llorella

The design concept of this apartment, located in a small village one hour outside of Barcelona, was primarily determined by the fan shape of the living area. Because of this layout, the center of the apartment receives inadequate light. So the decision was made to forgo any unnecessary interim walls in the core area and to situate the kitchen and eating area in the space thereby created. In order to allow the light to penetrate the interior, the custom-made kitchenette/dividing wall was restricted to a height of five feet. The lightness of this design is emphasized by the white color of the facings, ceilings, and walls, and accentuated the black work surfaces and the decorative extractor hood. The long ceiling niche, also in black, was used for a linear array of spots. This open concept is also used in the design of the living room, which extends seamlessly from the kitchen area. Indeed, here the cool atmosphere of the apartment was warmed up with the combination of oak flooring and brown furnishings and fittings.

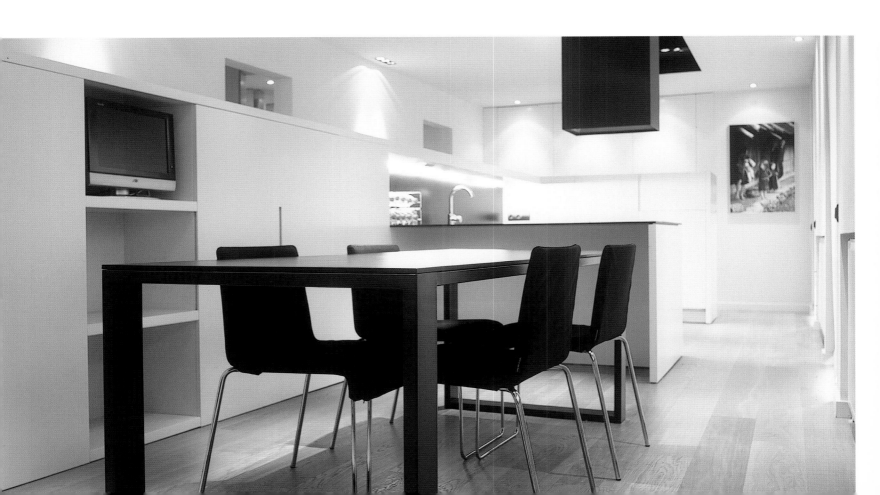

To combat a lack of natural light, the structure of the entrance area was designed to do away with any unnecessary interim walls, though some could not be removed due to their supporting function.

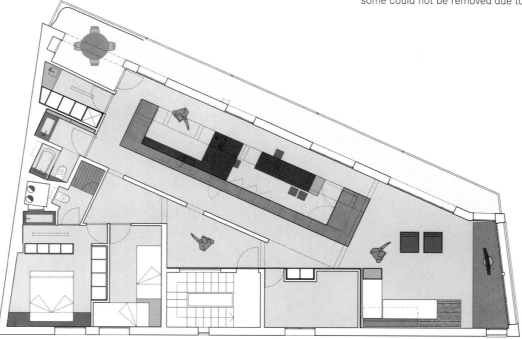

Plan

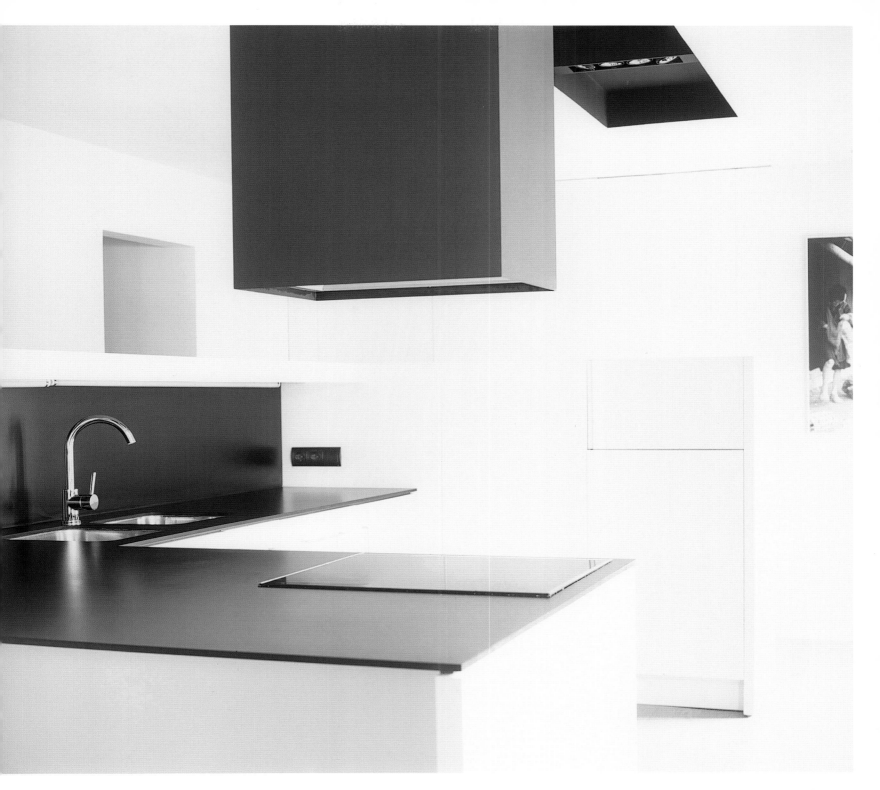

The summery, open design of the kitchen is emphasized by the whiteness of the cabinet fronts, ceilings, and walls.

The living room extends continously from the kitchen area. Here, in contrast to the stark kitchen, the combination of brown furnishings with white walls creates a warm atmosphere.

To maintain an airy atmosphere, the parents' bedroom was kept completely white. In contrast, the children's bedrooms were enriched with wooden furniture, wall drawings, and colorful fittings.

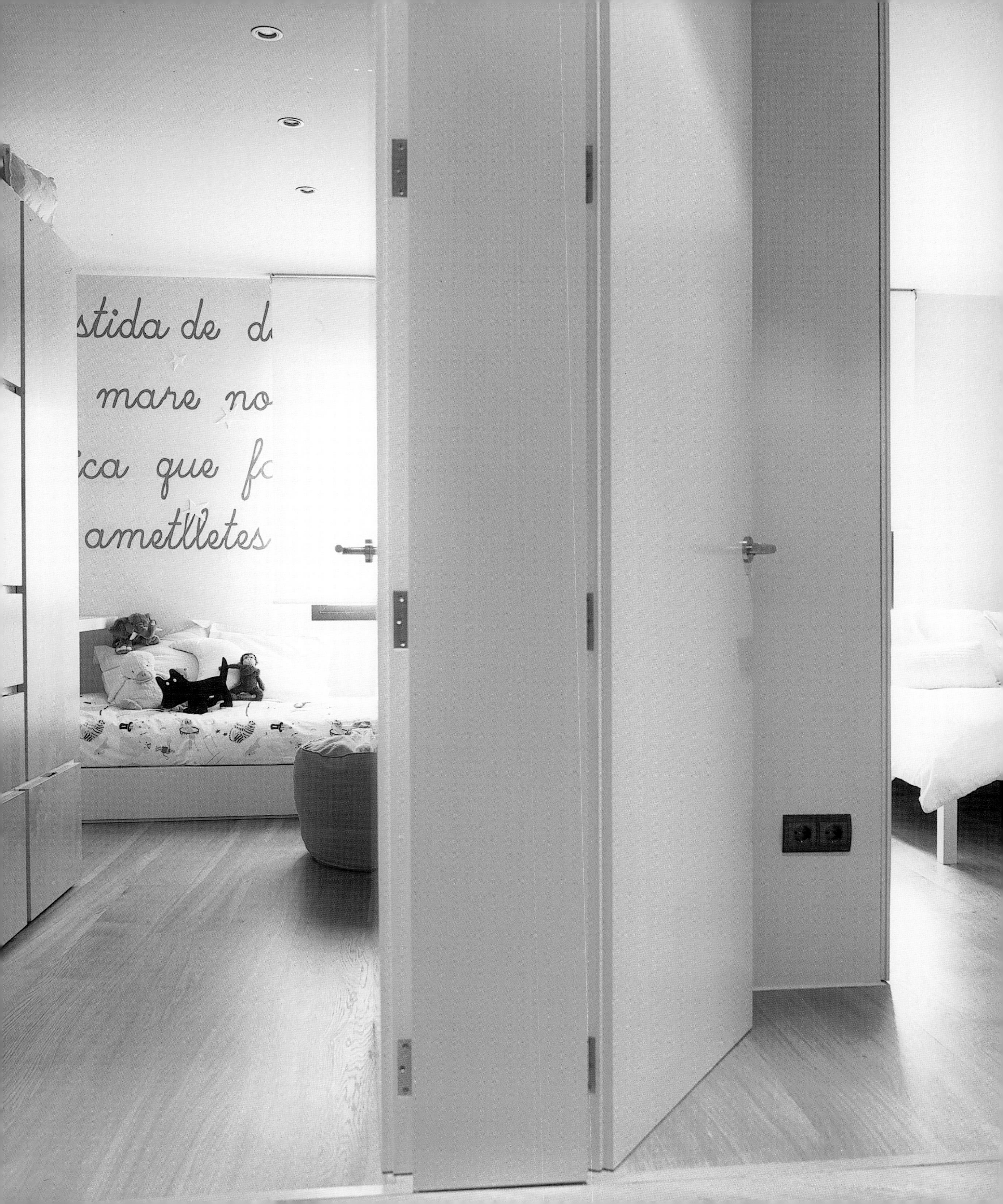
stida de
mare no
ca que
ametlletes

Lisbon Apartment

Location Lisbon, Portugal **Photography** © Fernando and Sérgio Guerra

In designing this apartment in Lisbon, the architect, João Santa-Rita, placed particular importance on the correspondence between the exterior and the interior. With a view to the near Pedro de Alcântara Park and Castelo e da Graça hill, the apartment is located in the bustling district of Bairro Alto. Here the lively alley bars, restaurants, and shops are clustered in close proximity. João Santa-Rita brought this appealing, hilly landscape indoors by means of sculptural shapes in walls, shelves, or other structures. To highlight the effect of the unusual shapes, intense colors were eschewed.

The walls were painted white, which serves as a contrast to the dark wooden flooring, sliding doors, and wall cladding. Like flowers in a meadow, only the yellow, pink, and orange chairs offer accents of color in this environment, with its emphasis on shapes. The amorphous landscape is also complemented by sliding doors, which determine the relationships of the individual rooms, and which enable the hallway, in the center of the rectangular apartment, to receive some natural light.

The triangular corridor receives all of its sunlight by way of the room facing the street. In order to counterbalance the hallway's lack of windows, skylights were created and opaque glass strips were installed in the doors.

In addition to the sculptural walls, the furnishings and fittings were custom-made. Vivid color was not used, so as to keep the attention on the forms and shapes.

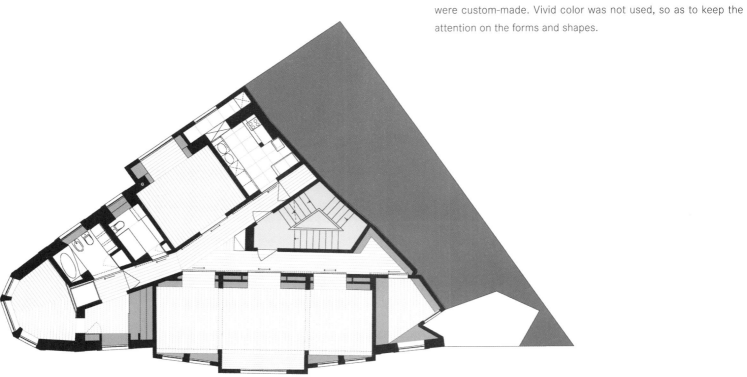

Plan

The contrast-rich black-and-white palette is enhanced in the bathroom by glossy surfaces that reflect the halogen spots and create an exciting atmosphere.

Mayfair Penthouse

SPENCE | HARRIS HOGAN ASSOCIATES

Location London, UK **Photography** © Francesca Yorke

This residence is located on the eighth floor of a 1960s apartment block built in the center of London. After thorough deliberations and extensive communication with the client, the architects decided against their first idea that of keeping the apartment's original structure and modernizing only by changing the furnishings and fittings. Ultimately they decided on a complete revamp of the space. To create an airier atmosphere, the ceilings, floors, and walls were removed and completely reconfigured. The kitchen and living room were made open and continuous. The stainless-steel kitchen was raised on a platform; it differentiates itself from the living room further by a light Pietro Lara floor. The living room's dark brown walnut floor combines harmoniously with the beige sofa and vintage leather chairs. The library serves as a boundary of this space, with a work table that can be concealed in the shelf and an original Arne Jacobsen Egg chair. The design of the bedroom also deserves attention. Under the bed, which floats in the air, speakers and colorful disco lights were installed.

The kitchen and living room were designed to flow into one another. The stainless-steel kitchen was raised on a platform and further differentiates itself from the living room with light Pietro Lara flooring.

Behind the kitchen end of the living area are the master bedroom and bathroom – one of the most extraordinary spaces in the house. The bath is bespoke dark grey limestone, set within a white Pietro Lara stone floor, with the same stone used for the basins, for maximum contrast.

The bedroom décor deserves particular attention. Under the bed, which floats in the air, speakers and disco lights were installed; the lights change colors in time with the music.

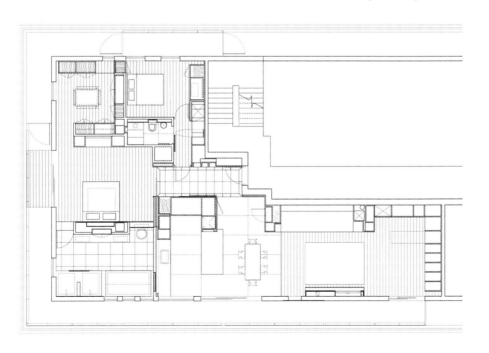

Plan

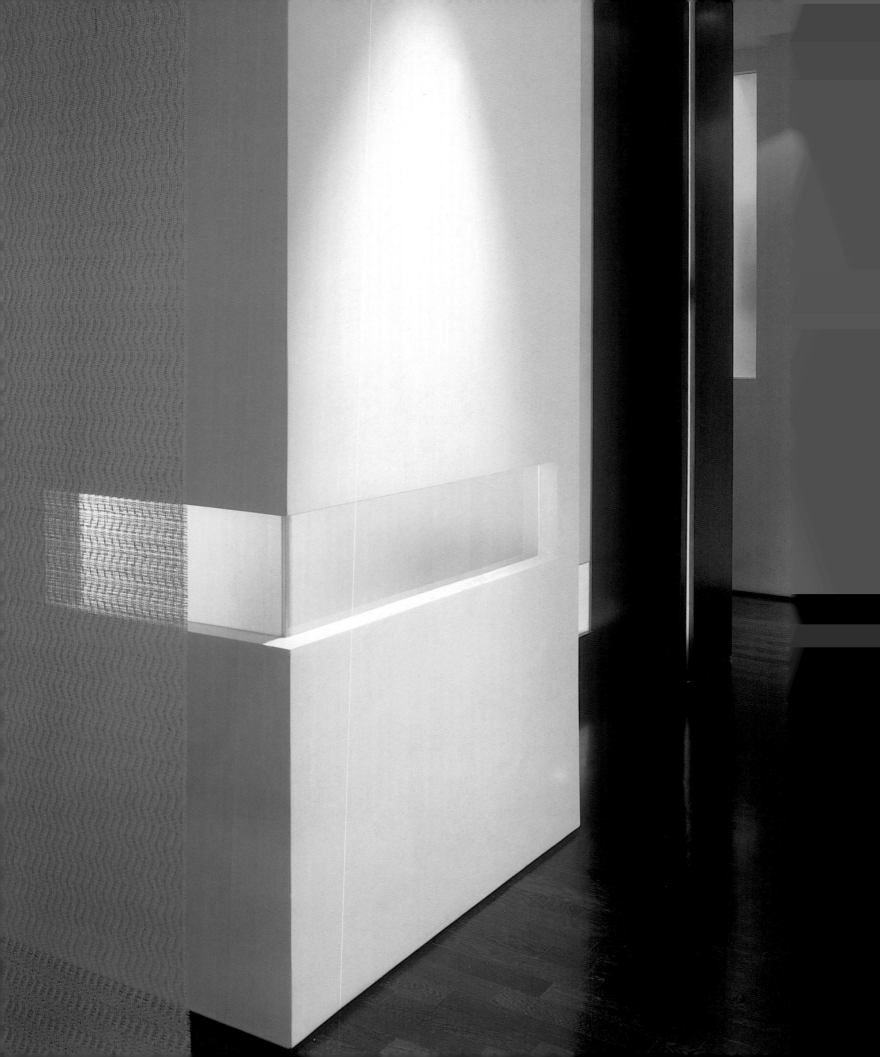

M. B. House

Location Rome, Italy **Photography** © Luigi Filetici

Warm tones such as brown, beige, and white, along with crystal bands partially backlit in a fresh shade of turquoise, are skillfully combined to create a friendly and dynamic Roman-style attic apartment. To allow flexible room configurations, the architect innovatively used movable cellular fabric panels by Woodnotes to separate or join the living room, dining room, and kitchen as needed. To make the best use of the available space, no corridor exists; the entrance area, partially protected by a closet, leads directly into the living room. A special focal point here is the handcrafted wall cladding and a long wooden bench made of dark oak. The front of this furniture was draped in linen in order to conceal the sound system located below it. The dining room table was also finished in dark oak wood, thereby visually linking the living room and the kitchen. Playing upon the unusual turquoise light bands, a blue crystalline lamp by the Fontana Arte company was installed here, coherently rounding out the overall concept.

A special feature of the living room is the hand-processed natural stone cladding; the long dark oak bench is linen fabric in order to conceal the hi-fi equipment from view.

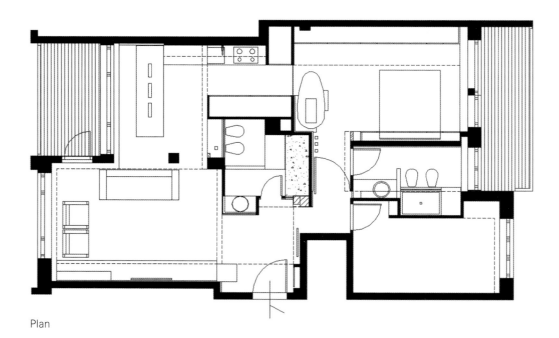

Plan

An innovative and appealing way to allow for flexible room reconfiguration is the use of Woodnotes' movable panels of cellular fibers that can separate or join the living room, dining room, and kitchen as needed.

A focal point of the bathroom is its freestanding bathtub that receives not only water but also rays of light from above. This stylish lighting design is complemented by glass bands lit from behind.

You and Me

Location Barcelona, Spain **Photography** © Nuria Fuentes, special thanks to Casa Decor 2005

This urban dwelling, designed by the studio Casadesús for the company Cosentino as part of an interior design trade show, Casa Decor 2005, plays upon the avant-garde and the traditional. The concept's starting point is a 1,400-square-foot apartment in a historic art-nouveau house that was to be converted into a residence and work space for a young couple. The result is an eclectic design in which the existing period elements are combined with geometric, contemporary furnishings, fittings, and industrial materials. Especially in the studio—originally the kitchen—this idea of combining recycled elements with modern furnishings and fittings can be seen. For example, the old coal-burning stove serves as a pedestal for the central worktable of Silestone slabs. Such contrast is further emphasized by the dominance of the colors black and white. Meanwhile, the current kitchen area, situated in the open living space, serves as a visual barrier between the workshop and sleeping area. The industrial aesthetic of the concrete flooring is highlighted by the use of plastic pipes that conceal plumbing under the sink.

The kitchen extends into the open living area. The adjacent dining
table can also be used as a work surface, which saves space. This
entire area is visually unified by means of the lamps that hang from
the ceiling in a long line.

Prohibido estacionar. Gra

Si	No
- anar al cine	- anar al gimnàs
- menjar "xuxes"	- menjar verdures
- mirar la tele	fruita, peix,
- anar de compres	llegums cereals
- llevar-me tard	- fer la compra
- fumar i beure	- anar de vacances
- fer el "vago"	- arribar puntual
	a la feina

T Y
U O

Despite the eclectic combination of historic and modern elements, such as antique mirrors with contemporary fixtures, the interior design does not appear flamboyant. This is because the color palette was restricted to basic black and white.

Especially in the studio—originally the kitchen—the idea of combining recycled items with modern furnishings can be seen. The old coal-burning stove now serves as a pedestal for the central worktable.

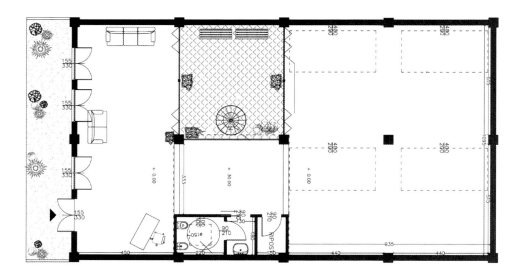

Plan

Ample Street Apartment

Location Barcelona, Spain **Photography** © Gogortza & Llorella

For this apartment, located in a historic eighteenth century building, the challenge was to modernize the structure—thereby improving the use of space—while at the same time designing the various bedrooms as possible rentals. Consequently, the rooms used in common were designed to be spacious and to connect to one another. To honor the history of the apartment despite its updated modern feel, the original ceiling height was maintained and the beams were restored. A pass-through to the kitchen and an open corridor enable continuous communication. In fact, the opening was designed as a kitchen bar to make more effective use of this area. The bedrooms, completely equipped with bathrooms and closets, extend off a long hallway. Since the hallway receives very little natural light, drop ceiling and square lamps were installed, and the vivid orange wall also contributes to the bright, friendly ambience. In contrast is the monochromatic color palette of the white walls and black doors, which were jazzed up with such graphic elements as the large, white numbers.

To connect the kitchen with the communal living area, a pass-through was created; it also provides additional eating space near a dining table in the living room.

Since the corridor leading to the individual rooms does not receive any natural light, a drop ceiling and square lamps were installed; the orange wall provides a bright and colorful backdrop.

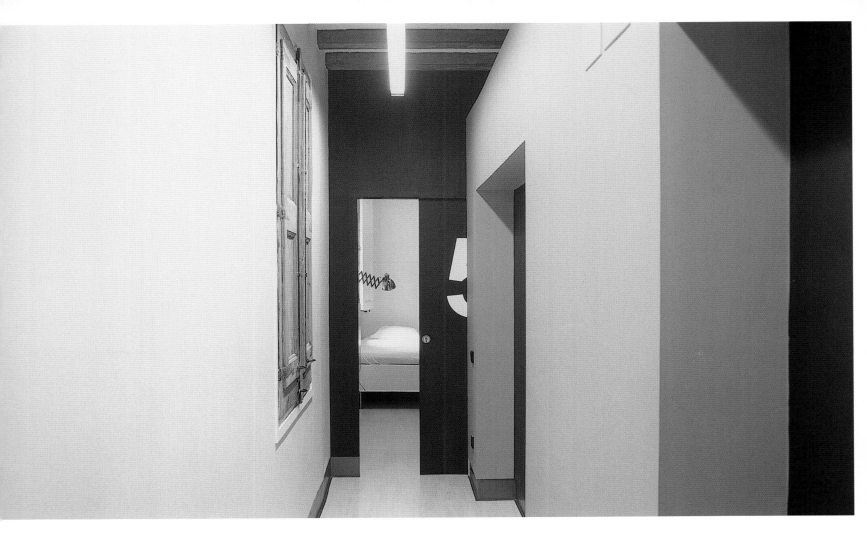

Functional and decorative at the same time, the large, white graphic numerals on the bedroom doors pop against the black paint.

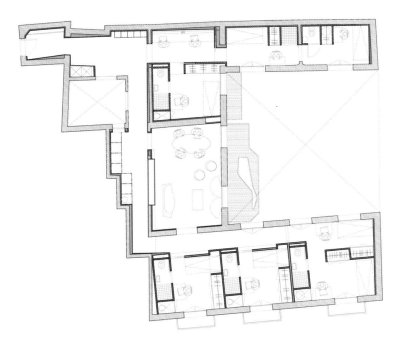

Plan

The sleek design carries over into the individual rooms, where black closets contrast with the white paint and the color scheme is livened up by the orange bathroom wall.

Apartment Abaixadors

Location Barcelona, Spain **Photography** © Gogortza & Llorella

This trapezoid-shaped loft is located very near a medieval church, Santa Maria del Mar, in the Born, the trendy district of Barcelona. In Mediterranean architecture, the living areas are built around a patio or areaway; this principle is echoed in this 700-square-foot residence. The traditional layout was maintained as the individual areas were distributed around the patio. In order to create an open and spacious ambience, all transverse-running elements were finished in transparent glass, allowing natural light to penetrate throughout. The glass-clad bathroom is particularly eye-catching: It projects on a platform from the dressing area. The floating effect thereby created is strengthened by lighting above and below. As a contrast to this transparent environment, the original brick walls were retained; a light well running along the floor emphasizes the texture. The wooden ceiling beams and arches were also restored, imbuing the minimalist, contemporary furnishings with the rich history of the location.

As a counterpoint to the open layout of the apartment, the building's original brick walls were retained; a light well running along the floor enhances their texture.

The kitchen took the form of a box in the living room; it was encased in glass panels that admit natural light but contain odors.

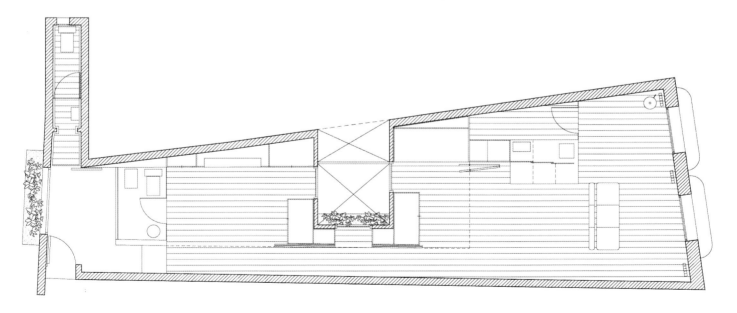

Plan

A special feature of the wooden clad bedroom is the glassed-in bathroom that projects on a platform from the dressing area. The floating effect thereby created is reinforced by illumination from above and below.

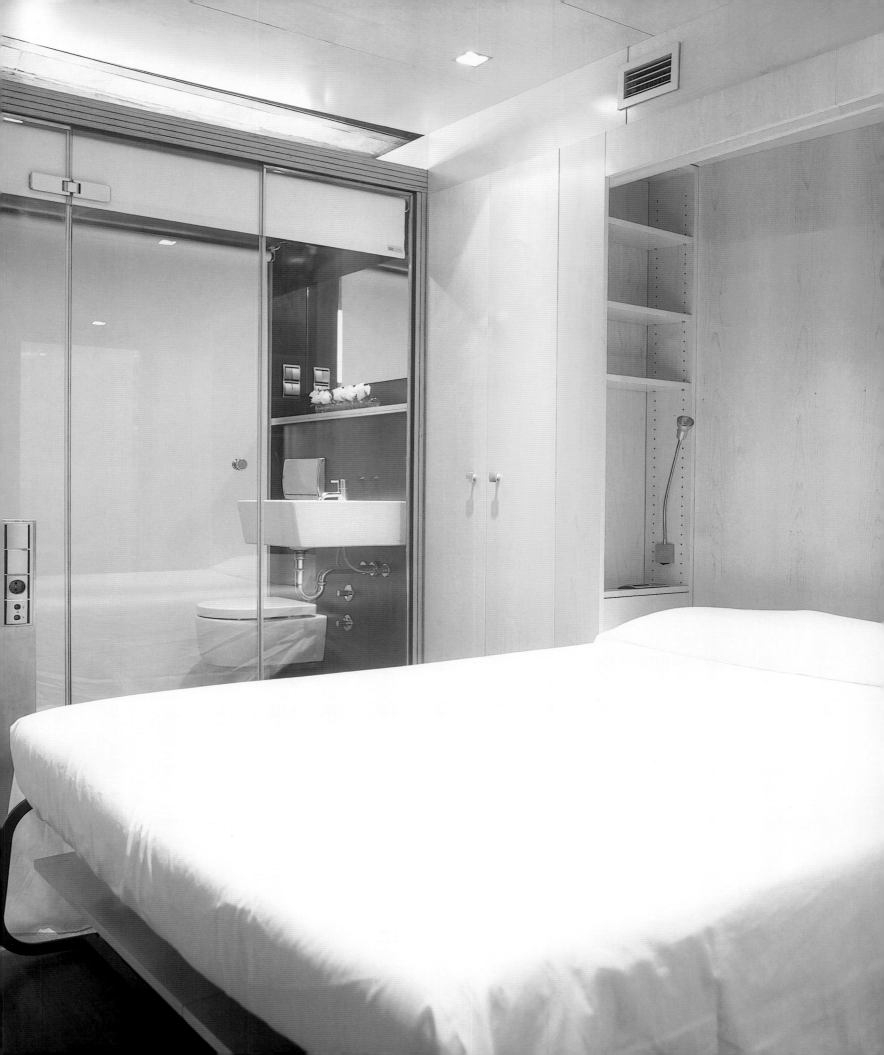

Directory

AAGF estudio, Grupo CRU
Av. Generalitat 26, 08754 El Papiol, Barcelona, Spain
Tel.: 34 936 731 686
Fax: 34 936 730 725
cru@cru2001.com
www.grupcru.com

Air Projects
Pau Claris 179, 3º 1ª, 08037 Barcelona, Spain
Tel.: 34 932 722 427
Fax: 34 932 722 428
air@air-projects.com
www.air-projects.com

Arantxa Garmendia, David Maturen
C/ Santa Isabel 3, ático, 5003 Zaragoza, Spain
Tel.: 34 976 392 407
Fax: 34 976 399 895
davidmaturen@hotmail.com

Architects EAT
Level 2, 227 Commercial Road, South Yarra, VIC 3141, Australia
Tel.: 61 3 9824 0813
Fax: 61 3 9824 0843
office@eatas.com.au
www.eatas.com.au

BBP Architects
7/25 Argyle Street, Fitzroy, VIC 3065, Australia
Tel.: 61 3 9416 1486
Fax: 61 3 9416 1438
info@bbparchitects.com
www.bbparchitects.com

B. E. Architecture
Studio 7 Level 6 289 Flinders Lane, Melbourne, VIC 3000, Australia
Tel.: 61 3 9650 6033
Fax: 61 3 9650 0133
info@bearchitecture.com
www.bearchitecture.com

Casadesús
C/Verge del Pilar 2, 2-1, 08750 Molins de Rei, Barcelona, Spain
Tel.: 34 936 684 760
Fax: 34 936 684 724
estudi@casadesusdisseny.com
www.casadesusdisseny.com

Cassandra Complex
51 O'Connell Street, North Melbourne, VIC 3051, Australia
Tel.: 61 3 9329 8308
Fax: 61 3 9329 8309
staff@cassandracomplex.com.au
www.cassandracomplex.com.au

Custom Espais
Paseo Mas Oliver 10, 1º, 08005 Barcelona, Spain
Tel.: 34 933 004 884
Fax: 34 933 007 250
customespais@coac.net
www.customespais.net

Delugan Meissl Associated Architects
Mittersteig 13/4, A-1040 Vienna, Austria
Tel.: 43 1 585 3690
Fax: 43 1 585 3690 11
office@deluganmeissl.at
www.deluganmeissl.at

Desai Chia Architecture
54 West 21st Street, Seventh Floor, New York, NY 10010, USA
Tel.: 1 212 366 9630
Fax: 1 212 366 9278
info@desaichia.com
www.desaichia.com

Eduard Samsó
C/ Tallers 77, ático, 08001 Barcelona, Spain
Tel.: 34 933 425 900
samso@coac.net

Estudio Interiorismo Adela Cabré
C/ Diputació 229, 08007 Barcelona, Spain
Tel.: 34 934 533 331
Fax: 34 934 533 352
adela@adelacabreinteriorismo.com
www.adelacabreinteriorismo.com

Filippo Bombace
3, Via Isola del Giglio, 00141 Rome, Italy
Tel./Fax: 39 06 86 89 82 66
info@filippobombace.com
www.filippobombace.com

Francesc Rifé
C/ Escuelas Pías 25, bajos, 08017 Barcelona, Spain
Tel.: 34 934 141 288
Fax: 34 932 412 814
f@rife-design.com
www.rife-design.com

Frank la Rivière
1-2-14, Setagaya, Setagaya-ku, Tokyo, 154-0017, Japan
Tel./Fax: 81 3 3428 4046
archi-f@t08.itscom.net
www.frank-la-riviere.com

Greek/Josep Mª Font
C/ Rubinstein 4, 08022 Barcelona, Spain
Tel.: 34 934 189 550
Fax: 34 934 189 532
greek@greekbcn.com
www.greekbcn.com

Hariri & Hariri Architecture
39 West 29th Street, 12th Floor, New York, NY 10001, USA
Tel.: 1 212 727 0338
Fax: 1 212 727 0479
info@haririandhariri.com
www.haririandhariri.com

Joan Jesús Puig de Ayguavives, collaboration: Claudia Rueda Velázquez
Consell de Cent 383, 1º 1ª, 08009 Barcelona, Spain
Tel.: 34 934 870 872
Fax: 34 935 288 141
jjpuig@coac.net

Josep Cano i Damunt
Plaza Can Felipa 3, 1º 3ª, 08005 Barcelona, Spain
Tel./Fax: 34 699 492 056
josepcano@loftbcn.com
www.loftbcn.com

LABB Arquitectura
Milà i Fontanals 14-26, 2-9, 08012 Barcelona, Spain
Tel.: 34 934 765 303
Fax: 34 934 765 304
cfernandez@labbnet.com
www.labbnet.com

La Granja
Ciutat de Granada 28 bis, 3ª, 08005 Barcelona, Spain
Tel.: 34 933 568 405
Fax: 34 933 568 406
info@lagranja.it
www.lagranja.it

M2-Nakatsuji Architect Atelier
1-3-5-601 Ebisu-Nishi, Shibuya-ku, Tokyo, 150-0021, Japan
Tel./Fax: 81 3 5459 0095
m-naka@mxj.mesh.ne.jp
www2u.biglobe.ne.jp/~m-naka/

Martínez Lapeña-Torres Arquitectes
C/ de Roca i Batlle 14, 12, 08023 Barcelona, Spain
Tel.: 34 932 121 416
Fax: 34 932 540 682
jamlet@arquired.es

Messana O'Rorke Architects
118 West 22nd Street, Ninth Floor, New York, NY 10011, USA
Tel.: 1 212 807 1960
Fax: 1 212 807 1966
brian@messanaororke.com
www.messanaororke.com

Millimetre
Level 1, 269 Spring Street, Melbourne, VIC 3000, Australia
Tel.: 61 3 9650 2523
Fax: 61 3 9650 2550
info@millimetre.com.au
www.millimetre.com.au

NAT Architecten
Generaal Vetterstraat 73B, 1059 BTR Amsterdam, Netherlands
Tel.: 31 20 67 90 750
Fax: 31 20 67 56 444
info@natarchitecten.nl
www.natarchitecten.nl

Pilar Líbano
Rambla de Catalunya 103, pal. B, 08008 Barcelona, Spain
Tel./Fax: 34 932 159 841
pilar@plibano.com

Plasma Studio
Unit 51, Regent Studios, 8 Andrews Road, London E8 4QN, UK
Tel.: 44 20 8985 5560
Fax: 44 87 0486 5563
info@plasmastudio.com
www.plasmastudio.com

SA Advanced, Pedro Mora, Marta Sánchez-Bedoya, Juan Ramón Rodríguez, Fernando Díaz
Ctra. GU-254 km 3,5, 19114 Moratilla de los Meleros, Guadalajara, Spain
Tel.: 34 949 388 717
Fax: 34 949 388 773

Santa-Rita Arquitectos
Rua Cidade de Nova Lisboa, "Quinta da Fonte do Anjo", Olivais, 1800-107 Lisbon, Portugal
Tel.: 351 21 84 85 555
Fax: 351 21 85 38 060
santaritaarq@sapo.pt

Search Architekten
Weissenburgstrasse 32, 70180 Stuttgart, Germany
Tel.: 49 711 640 06 80
Fax: 49 711 640 06 81
team@se-arch.de
www.se-arch.de

Spence Harris Hogan Associates
1 Vencourt Place, Ravenscourt Park, Hammersmith, London W6 9NU, UK
Tel.: 44 20 8600 4171
Fax: 44 20 8600 4181
info@shh.co.uk
www.shh.co.uk

Tang Kawasaki Studio
338 East 5th Street, No. 19, New York, NY 10003, USA
Tel./Fax: 1 212 614 9594
jason@tangkawasaki.com
www.tangkawasaki.com